Advance Praise for *The Ugly Duckling Goes to Work!*

"This book skillfully evokes both our imagination and our experience. I loved returning to these fables because I could feel my childlike curiosity reawaken. Under Mette's skillful guidance that curiosity became the means to reexamine many organizational and personal dynamics. I was challenged, stimulated, and ultimately saw many things in a new light."
—**Margaret J. Wheatley,** author, *Leadership and the New Science*

"Fascinating! Mette Norgaard has crafted a wonderful and thought-provoking connection between the wisdom of the classic tales of Hans Christian Andersen and her own deep understanding of the timeless principles that govern a rich and effective work life. Bravo, Mette!"
—**Douglas R. Conant,** President and CEO, Campbell Soup Co.

"This book offers real help with the task of finding fulfillment in the workplace. What Joseph Campbell did to help us understand the inner journey, Mette Norgaard does for the career path. The reader will be charmed as she applies the wisdom of enchanting stories to the challenges of our livelihoods."
—**Jonathan Young,** Ph.D., Psychologist, Founding Curator, Joseph Campbell Archives

"Great and unusual!! Mette Norgaard has connected those invaluable childhood lessons with the applications of adults—both business and personal! These stories give an entirely new perspective to the continuing evolution of these relationships and interactions! Well done!"
—**Horst H. Schulze,** Founding President and COO, The Ritz-Carlton Hotel Company, current President and CEO, The West Paces Hotel Group, LLC

THE UGLY DUCKLING
GOES TO WORK

■

Wisdom for the Workplace
from the Classic Tales of
Hans Christian Andersen

METTE NORGAARD

AMACOM

AMERICAN MANAGEMENT ASSOCIATION
New York · Atlanta · Brussels · Chicago · Mexico City
San Francisco · Shanghai · Tokyo · Toronto · Washington, D.C.

This publication is designed to provide accurate and authoritative
information in regard to the subject matter covered. It is sold with the
understanding that the publisher is not engaged in rendering legal,
accounting, or other professional service. If legal advice or other expert
assistance is required, the services of a competent professional person
should be sought.

Library of Congress Cataloging-in-Publication Data

Norgaard, Mette.
        The ugly duckling goes to work : wisdom for the workplace from the classic
tales of Hans Christian Andersen / Mette Norgaard.
            p.   cm.
        Includes bibliographical references and index.
        ISBN 0-8144-0871-0 (hardcover)
        1. Work—Miscellanea.   2. Andersen, H. C. (Hans Christian), 1805–1875—
Criticism and interpretation.   I. Andersen, H. C. (Hans Christian), 1805–
1875.   II. Title.

HD4904.N673   2005
650.1—dc22   2004024202

Printing Number

10   9   8   7   6   5   4   3   2   1

to Alfredo,
and his creativity, courage, and high standards

I shall come and sing for you,
so you may be joyful
—and thoughtful.

H. C. ANDERSEN, *THE NIGHTINGALE*

CONTENTS

FOREWORD

THIS BOOK HAS profound relevance as we transition from the control model of the Industrial Age to the release model of the Information/Knowledge Worker Age. I suggest that the biggest problem we have in most organizations and workplaces today is that we are still using the Industrial model while attempting to operate and compete in an Information/Knowledge Worker Age. Unless we adopt the mindset, skill set, and tool set associated with unleashing human potential, with helping people, and with finding our own voice and inspiring others to find theirs, we will become history. By contrast, those who successfully make the transition will make the future. This outcome is inevitable because it's pragmatic. Ironically, it is also idealistic. Thus the unique juxtaposition in Hans Christian Andersen's tales between the practical and the ideal parallels our present challenge.

Before I elaborate, let me a say a word about Mette Norgaard. For years, the executive development programs at the Covey Leadership Center and later FranklinCovey were graced by her presence, her leadership, and her teachings. She is one of the more caring, insightful, and truly effective teachers I have ever known. When you are around her, and even when her reflective thoughts and questions posed in this book surround you, you will sense that she did not just learn these magnificent insights—she *earned* them.

Mette, much like the nightingale in this book, has the quiet courage to sing her own song and to encourage (put courage into) others to find their own voice and sing their own song. As she discusses each tale and shares her personal convictions, it would seem we are studying Mette's personal journey, discoveries, and development. But when I read and reflected on this book, I felt as if I were also studying my own personal journey, discoveries, and development. Such is the power of poetic metaphor and parabolic teaching. Everyone comes at it from the lens and vector of one's own life.

As you truly reflect upon the stories in this book and discuss them with others, particularly with your own work team, the book's practical insights and idealistic motivations will help lubricate the necessary transformation. Let me give you a few "for instances."

The Emperor's New Clothes particularly illustrates a statement someone made—"When man found the mirror he began to lose his soul." The point is, he became more concerned with his image than with himself. I believe that you will find that over 90 percent of all leadership and personal failures are basically failures of character, and at the most fundamental level the tales in this book are all about character. This is extremely relevant in today's organizations, particularly business organizations, which are becoming guilty by association because of the scandals of a few. I believe those few are just the tip of an iceberg and that the great mass has not yet surfaced. These cultural flaws are essentially a fruit of the Industrial Age model, which nourished bureaucracies, hierarchies, competitive silos, kissing-up politics, hidden agendas, and denial, denial, denial.

The Ugly Duckling learned the hard way to find his own voice in harmony with nurturing swans and became freed from the metastasizing cancers of comparing and complaining and criticizing and contending—freed from the comparison-based identity that nurtures the codependency of the control model.

The Dung Beetle, obsessed with appearance and cleverness, is simply unaware of the horrible consequences of an inflated self-image. Arrogance, both personally and organizationally, is the main derailer of great performance.

The Nisse at the Grocer's displays a practical idealist who models the balance advocated by both Jim Collins and Peter Drucker, who essentially taught that the first duty of management is to face reality—the hard, cold, stubborn facts of reality—and then to be optimistic and opportunistic and idealistic.

The Fir Tree illustrates the dissatisfaction and frustration and futility of never living in the present. Not living in the present is futile because it violates the Law of the Harvest, where one must prepare the ground before planting, and also water, cultivate, weed, and nourish patiently, and then wait for nature to do its thing in making what's possible actual. You may be able to cram for an exam in school, but you cannot cram real growth.

The Nightingale is my favorite of all these tales because it epitomizes the integration of the practical and the idealistic. This is exactly what can happen in the workplace with a release model. Rather than the loneliness at the top of the Industrial Age organizations, where all the important decisions are made while the rest wield the screwdrivers, in Information/Knowledge Worker Age organizations leadership becomes distributed throughout the entire culture. Efforts become focused on helping people find or discover their strengths—their unique, natural talents. People become more willing to be part of a complementary team where strengths are made productive and weaknesses are made irrelevant through the strengths of others. It is a paradigm shift, as when the Copernican notion of the sun being at the center of the universe replaced the Ptolemaic concept that the earth was at the center.

This book, by helping us to understand the simple wisdom of Hans Christian Andersen, provides an absolutely apt and highly relevant metaphorical description of this paradigm shift, from a control-based to a release-based way of seeing ourselves and one another, and from a fragmented person to a whole person—body, mind, heart, and spirit. And, in my opinion, even though Mette wrote it for the workplace, the lessons are just as significant and relevant to the home place, the community place, and the privacy of one's own heart.

I hope you enjoy and gain from this material as much as I have. I commend it to you for discussion purposes in work teams and for training and development programs. Its humor will be a lubricant for humanizing and personalizing change!

Dr. Stephen R. Covey
Author of *The 7 Habits of Highly Effective People* and *The 8th Habit*

INTRODUCTION

■

Work can bring us alive, but it can also kill us.

IN MY INTERACTIONS with leaders I have noticed four persistent patterns. First, most professionals are ambitious, talented, and hard working. They are also savvy about the steps, rules, habits, and rituals for success. Moreover, they relentlessly push themselves to become ever better managers, leaders, spouses, parents, and athletes. These three patterns keep them so busy that they lead to a fourth one: They rarely slow down, reflect, and connect to their essential way of being, their inner wisdom.

This book is for people who want to make smart *and* wise choices, who want a comfortable standard of living *and* a good quality of life. It is for those who want to feel alive in their work, who want a work *life*.

While this book invites you to consider substantive questions about the meaning of life and work, it does so in a lighthearted manner. Rather than studying Plato or Descartes, we will learn from an ugly duckling, a gnome-like "nisse," and a nightingale. Instead of interpreting Dante and Shakespeare, we will explore the lives of a vain emperor, a swaggering dung beetle, and a restless fir tree. That is, we will use fairy tales as a way to understand human nature. For centuries elders have used fairy tales to speak to the dilemmas and conflicts of everyday life, to help us understand our need for meaning and deal with life's painful surprises.

I was born and raised in Denmark, so Hans Christian Andersen's fairy tales were an integral part of my upbringing. In my home, the 150th anniversary edition of his fairy tales was kept right next to the twelve-volume encyclopedia. It was a weighty book, with a leather spine and gold-rimmed pages, and it was handled with affection and respect. In the evenings, after we kids were cleaned up and ready for bed, the volume would be taken down and my father would read to us. My favorites then were the simple tales like *The Princess and the Pea* and *The Swineherd*, but other tales saddened, frightened, or disturbed me. Only as an adult did I begin to appreciate the depth of these stories. Where I before had been in tears over the little mermaid's demise, I now understood the beauty of unconditional love. Where I thought little Claus's behavior (*Little Claus and Big Claus*) was deceitful and nasty, I now saw a "little guy" outwitting a tyrant. I discovered what every Dane knows, that Andersen's stories were written for both children and adults.

Over the years, my appreciation for the author has continued to grow. As I began to study Andersen scholars, I understood why, as there is a clear pattern to his writing. Andersen's "heroes" are authentic, congruent, and real; his "villains" are narrow-minded, self-satisfied, and smug; and his hope for us is that we enjoy every moment and also grow into the person we were meant to be. Such a philosophy is close to my own heart and work.

During his formative years, the young Andersen spent hours listening to the old women tell folk tales in the spinning room where his grandmother worked, and his early stories were inspired by those tales. His most beautiful and complex stories, though, integrate this folk wisdom with his own experience and imagination.

Unfortunately, in the Anglo-American world most people are unfamiliar with the depth of Andersen's writing. Having pigeonholed him as a quaint, Victorian-era children's author, they have been deprived of his insights and wit. I hope my new translations and the discussions in this book will help remedy that. Because, in my experience, an emperor's heavy-handed use of power and a fir tree's restlessness are deeply relevant to the twenty-first century workplace.

To help the readers see Andersen as we Danes do, I shall use the name H. C. Andersen throughout the rest of this book. In Denmark we never call him Hans Christian Andersen. Using his first name would seem too familiar, but simply calling him Andersen would not work either, as we have too many of them. To us, he is always H. C. Andersen.

The book is organized into six independent chapters, each based on one of H. C. Andersen's classic tales. You can approach these chapters in sequence or simply start with those that interest you the most.

Three of the tales are cautionary (*The Emperor's New Clothes*, *The Dung Beetle*, and *The Fir Tree*), and they show us the consequences of being overly concerned with other people's opinions, rewards, and recognition. The other three tales are inspirational (*The Ugly Duckling*, *The Nisse at the Grocer's*, and *The Nightingale*), and they deal with the topics of longing, balance, and professional mastery. The first group of issues is largely pragmatic and requires *doing*, and the second is essentially idealistic and concerns *being*. Part of the lesson is that neither one should be carried too far, or we may spin off into mindless activity or become excessively self-absorbed.

Pragmatism and idealism are both useful when they complement each other. Today, however, other people's expectations tend to overwhelm our deepest interests. Many even dismiss their longings as being impractical and feel more accountable for the corporation's goals than for their own potential. If that is your situation, it is time to bring a little wisdom to your work.

Each chapter is structured the same way, giving you a choice in how to approach the stories. After a few introductory paragraphs, you can read either the brief Summary or the entire Classic Tale before you proceed to my commentary, titled The Tale at Work. If you choose to read the summary because you want to get to the work-related comments more quickly, you can always return to the full tale at your leisure.

You may approach this book in a relaxed manner and just enjoy each chapter. You could also choose to get more involved and contemplate the issues raised in the text. Incidentally, your conclusions from each tale may be different from mine; this often happens in workshops and in my discussions with family and friends, for each of us have learned different lessons about human nature and life.

The stories also offer a fun way to address tough issues with your colleagues. For example, *The Emperor's New Clothes* makes it possible to talk about what things are "undiscussable" on one's work team, and *The Ugly Duckling* enables us to talk about how we can encourage one another's strengths. Accordingly, at the end of each chapter I suggest a couple of topics for group discussion.

My passion is helping individuals to be authentic and alive in their work and helping create workplaces that make room for people's best energy. H. C. Andersen's tales are an inspiration as they show us how to release life rather than control it.

I invite you to bring H. C. Andersen with you to work. You don't need to tuck the tales under your arm and skip along the corporate corridors reciting *The Ugly Duckling*. You can simply let the tales inspire you to bring more meaning, more energy, and more joy to your work—to create or improve your work life.

WHY NEW TRANSLATIONS?

Within each chapter you will find my own translations of H. C. Andersen's tales. This is meant to remedy the many shortcomings of earlier renditions. Traditionally, much of the humor and rich detail in H. C. Andersen's tales has disappeared in English versions. Early English translators had little knowledge of Danish, so they translated from already existing German texts. To compound the problem, they freely edited the text to fit Victorian-era sensibilities, deleting many of H. C. Andersen's sharp and pointed comments. The translator's challenges persist to this day, though they are different. Current publishers often want to give the 150-year-old texts an easy flow and a contemporary feeling. Let me give just two examples.

In *The Emperor's New Clothes* the charlatans prey on people's fear that they may be seen as "unfit for [their] position or impermissibly stupid." The direct translation of the original Danish words "utilladelig dum" is "impermissibly stupid," which is unusual in English. So translators in the past have used "inadmissibly," "incorrigibly," "unforgivably," or "hopelessly" stupid. But the original "utilladelig dum" is also an unusual choice in Danish. To me, H. C. Andersen's intentionally strange choice almost suggests that we may come across *permissible* stupidity in our life, but then there is real stupidity, which is *impermissible*.

A more serious problem with contemporary translations is that they may even change the meaning of the original text. For example, in *Hans Christian Andersen: The Complete Fairy Tales and Stories* (1974) the translation of *The Dung Beetle* makes two intolerant frogs sound merely critical. One frog would like to know:

. . . if the swallow, who travels a good deal in foreign countries, ever has been in a land that has a better climate than ours. As much rain as you need; and a bit of wind, too—not to talk of the mist and the dew. Why, it is as good as living in a ditch. If you don't love this climate, then you don't love your country.

My more faithful translation reveals what the frog really wants to know:

. . . if the swallow who flies so far and wide, if it, on one of its many trips abroad, has found a better climate than ours. *Such gusts and such wetness!* It's just as if one were lying in a *wet* ditch! If that doesn't make one happy, well then one *certainly* doesn't love one's homeland!" [emphasis added]

The second translation is more accurate, showing us how H. C. Andersen engages the senses to make us really feel the wet and windy morning. But what is more essential is the nuance of the word *certainly*, without which the sentence is just an observation, rather than the self-righteous statement that H. C. Andersen meant it to be. We come across this when we hear statements like, "She *certainly* is gone a lot." "He *certainly* isn't a team player."[1]

H. C. Andersen was often the recipient of such judgmental attitudes. In particular, he was faulted for being overly fond of traveling and having too many German friends. With the exchange between two self-satisfied and smug frogs, he gives the reader the opportunity to ponder, "Could there be an intolerant frog in me?" Fortunately, Andersen keeps it light, avoids preaching and moralizing, and quickly moves on to a new vignette.

My aim in these translations has been to maintain H. C. Andersen's own style and choice of words whenever possible. As a consequence, while you may find some of the wording unusual and even slightly awkward at times, I trust you will appreciate the freshness and insights gained in exchange.

1

THE EMPEROR'S
NEW CLOTHES

■

When we seek to fit in,
we adopt other people's agenda.

■

"MANY YEARS AGO there lived an Emperor, who was so exceedingly fond of beautiful new clothes that he spent all his money on being well dressed." With this opening line, the story captures how vanity can make us look great and act silly at the same time.

H. C. Andersen does not criticize us for playing a particular role or cultivating a certain look. He himself was quite dapper and adept at managing his image.

What does bother H. C. Andersen is pretense. This prickly little tale is his way of poking fun at phoniness and snobbery, at how we, in order to be accepted, will pretend to appreciate things we do not agree with or understand.

As you read the following summary or, if you prefer, the full tale, consider these questions: What intrigues you about the tale? What bothers you? Does it remind you of times when you behaved foolishly because of ego or fear?

A SUMMARY OF THE TALE

The Emperor was so fond of clothes that he did not care about anything else. Just as one might say that a King was in the council chamber, so it was said here: "The Emperor is in his wardrobe."

One day, two charlatans arrived. They claimed they could weave the most magnificent cloth, which had the strange quality of being invisible to everyone who was "unfit for his position" or "impermissibly stupid." The Emperor thought this would be a great way for him to tell who could not handle his position and who was unwise, and he ordered the cloth be made at once.

All the people knew of the strange power of the cloth, and all were impatient to see how inept or dim-witted their neighbors were.

After some time, the Emperor wondered about the progress on the cloth. Feeling a little uneasy about its strange power, he first sent a trusted minister and later another affable official to check the work. Neither could see a thing, for there was nothing there. Each wondered, "Could I be stupid?" "Could I be unsuited for my position?" But they wanted no one to find out, so they effusively praised the fine colors and pattern.

A few days later, the Emperor arrived with his entourage to see for himself. "What's this!" thought the Emperor, "I can't see anything! Am I stupid? Am I no good at being Emperor?" But to make sure no one would find out, he exclaimed, "Oh, it's most beautiful!"

The whole entourage also looked and looked, but made no more of it than the others. "It is *magnifique!* Exquisite! Excellent!" it went from mouth to mouth, and they advised the Emperor to have new clothes made for the upcoming procession.

The night before the procession the charlatans acted as if they were busy cutting the fabric and sewing the new clothes, and in the morning they asked the Emperor to remove all his garments and "dressed" him in the new clothes.

Along the procession route the people cheered and applauded. Never had the Emperor's clothes been such a success. But suddenly a little child said, "But he doesn't have anything on!" and people began to whisper to one another that a child had said "He doesn't have anything on!" Soon everyone shouted, "But he doesn't have anything on!"

The Emperor shuddered, for it seemed to him they were right. Still, he had to see the procession through, and that he did.

DID YOU KNOW ... In 1837 H. C. Ander-

sen published his third pamphlet of tales. It included the tragic fairy tale *The Little Mermaid* and the witty story *The Emperor's New Clothes*.

His two first pamphlets had been given a lukewarm reception. In the introduction to the third pamphlet, H. C. Andersen writes that people had found the fairy tales to be "highly unimportant" and advised him not to continue writing them. He further noted that "a poet is always a poor man in his own little country. Fame is therefore the golden bird he has to catch! Time will tell if I catch it by telling fairy tales." Well, time did tell. Not only did he invent a new literary genre, transforming written Danish in the process, he also achieved the fame and immortality he craved all his life.

The Emperor's New Clothes was inspired by a fourteenth-century Spanish story by Infante Don Juan Manuel published in *El Conde Lucanor* (1335), a collection of instructive tales based on Jewish and Arabic stories. In the Middle Ages, birth instead of merit determined one's destiny. Therefore, in this earlier tale the swindlers' ruse was that if you could not see the cloth, your father was not who you thought he was. A person seen to be illegitimate would lose his name, position, and inheritance.

The King liked this idea, for if someone were declared a bastard, the property would default to the crown. So, imagine the King's horror when, instead of getting a windfall, he discovered that he could not see the cloth himself. Was he not the legitimate heir to the kingdom?

In the end, an African, who did not know or care about his father, told the King that he was stark naked. After the King admitted his folly, everyone set out to try to catch the swindlers, but they were long gone.

THE CLASSIC TALE

MANY YEARS AGO *there lived an Emperor who was so exceedingly fond of beautiful new clothes that he spent all his money on being well dressed. He cared little for his soldiers, and he did not enjoy plays or drives in the woods unless it was to show off his new clothes. He had an outfit for every hour of the day, and as you would say about a King that "he's in the council chamber," so it was always said here that "the Emperor's in his wardrobe."*

The great city where he lived was very enjoyable. Every day many visitors came, and one day two charlatans arrived. They pretended to be weavers and said that they knew how to weave the finest cloth one could imagine. Not only were the colors and pattern uncommonly beautiful, but the clothes made from the fabric had the strange quality that they would be invisible to every person who was unfit for his position or impermissibly stupid.

"These would be wonderful clothes," thought the Emperor. "By wearing them I could find out which men in my realm were inept at their work; I could tell the wise from the dumb! Yes, this cloth must be woven for me right away!" And he put a lot of money into the hands of the two impostors so they could begin their work.

They then put up two looms and pretended to work, but they had absolutely nothing on the looms. Bluntly they demanded the finest silk and the purest gold, and they stuck it all into their purses and worked with the empty looms late into the night.

"I wonder how far they have come with the cloth!" thought the Emperor. But he felt quite uneasy when he thought how anyone who was stupid or unfit for his position could not see it. He did not think he himself had anything to be afraid of. Even so, he would send someone else first to see how things were going. Everyone in the whole city knew of the strange power the cloth had, and everyone wanted to see how incompetent or dimwitted his neighbor was.

"I will send my honest old minister to the weavers," thought the Emperor. "He can best judge how the cloth looks, for he is intelligent and no one looks after his position better than he does!"

So the harmless old minister went into the hall where the two charlatans sat and worked on the empty looms.

"Dear God!" thought the old minister, opening his eyes wide. "I can't see a thing!" But he didn't say that.

Both charlatans invited him to step closer and asked him if it was not a beautiful pattern with lovely colors. Then they pointed to the empty loom, and the poor old minister continued to open his eyes wide, but he couldn't see a thing, for there was nothing there. "Dear God!" he thought. "Could I be stupid? I never would have thought so, and no one must know! Could I be unsuited for my position? No, it will never do for me to say that I can't see the cloth!"

"Well, you're not saying anything!" said the one who was weaving.

"Oh, it's beautiful. Quite charming!" said the old minister, looking through his glasses. "Such pattern and colors! Yes, I shall tell the Emperor that I am very pleased!"

"Well, we're glad to hear that!" said both weavers, and then they described the colors by name and the strange pattern. The old minister paid close attention so he could say the same thing when he came home to the Emperor. And that he did.

Then the charlatans demanded more money, more silk, and more gold for the weaving. They put everything into their own pockets while on the loom there was not a single thread. But they continued as before, weaving on the empty loom.

Soon after, the Emperor sent another harmless official to see how the weaving was coming along and whether the cloth would be finished soon. As with the minister, the official looked and looked, but since there was nothing but the empty looms, he could not see a thing.

"Yes, isn't it a beautiful piece of cloth?" said both charlatans, as they showed and explained the lovely pattern that wasn't there at all.

"Stupid I'm not!" thought the man. "Then it must be that I'm unfit for my important position. That's strange enough, but no one must notice!" And then he praised the cloth he didn't see and assured them that he was delighted with the beautiful colors and the lovely pattern. "Yes, it's most charming!" he said to the Emperor.

Everyone in the city talked about the magnificent cloth.

Soon the Emperor wanted to see it for himself while it was still on the loom. With an entourage of carefully selected men— among them the two harmless old officials who had been there before—he went to visit the sly impostors, who were now weaving at full speed without a thread or yarn.

"Yes, isn't it magnifique?" said both harmless officials. "Will your majesty look—what pattern, what colors!" And then they pointed to the empty loom, for they thought that everyone else could see the cloth.

"What's this!" thought the Emperor. "I can't see a thing! This is terrible! Am I stupid? Am I no good at being Emperor? This is the most horrible thing that could happen to me!" But he said, "Oh, it's most beautiful! It has my highest approval!" Then he nodded in a satisfied manner and looked at the empty loom. He did not want to say that he couldn't see a thing. The entourage he had brought along looked and looked, but were not able to make more of it than all the others. But they all said, like the Emperor, "Oh, it's most beautiful," and they advised him to wear the magnificent new clothes for the first time in the upcoming great procession. "It is magnifique! Exquisite! Excellent!" it went from mouth to mouth. And everyone was extremely pleased with it. The Emperor gave each of the charlatans a medal to hang from his buttonhole and the title of "Weaver-Squire."

The impostors were up all through the night before the morning of the procession, and they had more than sixteen candles lit. People could see they were busy finishing the Emperor's new clothes. They pretended to take the cloth from the loom, they cut in the air with big scissors, they sewed with needles without thread, and finally they said, "Look, now the clothes are finished!"

The Emperor himself came with his most distinguished gentlemen-in-waiting, and both charlatans held up an arm as if they were holding something, and then said, "Look, these are the breeches! Here's the coat! And here's the cloak!" And so forth. "It's as light as spider webs! You would think that you have nothing on your body, but that's precisely the beauty of it!"

"Yes," said the gentlemen-in-waiting, but they could not see a thing, for there was nothing there.

"If your imperial majesty would most graciously take off his clothes," said the charlatans, "then we can dress you in the new ones here in front of the big mirror!"

The Emperor took off all his clothes, and the charlatans acted as if they handed him each of the pieces they should have sewn. They reached around his waist as if they were tying something—that was the train—and the Emperor twisted and turned in front of the mirror.

"My, how well it suits you! How well it fits!" they all said. "What pattern! What colors! It's a precious outfit!"

"They're waiting outside with the canopy that will be carried over your majesty in the procession," said the chief master of ceremonies.

"Yes, I'm all ready!" said the Emperor. "Doesn't it fit well?" And then he turned one more time in front of the mirror, so it would seem like he was looking at his finery.

The gentlemen-in-waiting, who were to carry the train, fumbled with their hands along the floor as if they picked up the train, and they walked holding the air. They did not dare to let it be known that they could not see a thing.

Then the Emperor walked in the procession under the beautiful canopy. And all the people in the street and at the windows said, "My, the Emperor's new clothes are magnificent! What a beautiful train he has on that coat! And what an incredible fit!" No one would let it be noticed that he could not see anything, for then he would have been unfit for his position or very stupid. Never before had the Emperor's clothes been such a success.

"But he doesn't have anything on," said a little child. "Dear God, listen to the voice of the innocent," said the father; and then someone whispered to the next person what the child had said.

"He doesn't have anything on! There's a little child who says he doesn't have anything on!"

"But he doesn't have anything on!" everyone finally shouted. And the Emperor shuddered, for it seemed to him that they were right. But he thought, "I have to see the procession through." And he then carried himself even more proudly, and the gentlemen-in-waiting followed carrying the train that wasn't there at all.

THE TALE AT WORK

The Emperor's New Clothes is cited when people buy into a clever sales pitch instead of trusting their own judgment. Or when they, because of fear, say one thing publicly while they privately think something else. In both cases, we imply that people should face the facts and have the courage to speak the truth. Of course, this is easier said than done. As human beings we are genetically wired to avoid rejection. For millennia we needed the tribe to survive, and being ostracized meant losing one's identity and life. To prevent such a fate, even today we collaborate and form loyalties while we also compete for our place in the clan.

As we will see, fitting in is natural. As social beings, we enjoy relationships simply for their own sake (having a good time), but when we become too practical, when we manage our careers, relationships can become merely transactional, a means to an end (playing our role and playing it safe). Fitting in, however, has a shadow side. We may develop an oversized ego and mistake fawning for facts. Or we may completely dismiss or ignore the facts to maintain our position and reputation. The solution is simple but painful: We need to stop the deceptions and be descriptive. We need to name what is going on, at least to ourselves.

FITTING IN IS NATURAL

We fit into a group or a culture when we play by its rules and go along with its view of success, whether the group is a family, club, church, lifestyle enclave, corporate culture, or nation.

Fitting in is natural, and we figure out how to do it before we are eight years old. We know how to color within the lines, get gold stars, and gain the approval of our parents and teachers. We also remember the pain of rejection. We need only to listen to children when others do not want to play with them, or to teens who are not invited to a party, and we instantly recall our own traumas. Today, we may feel a similar twinge of rejection when we are excluded from an important meeting.

According to recent brain-scan studies, the pain of being excluded is as acute as physical injury. In a series of simple experiments, three "students" (a subject and two virtual players) played a video game tossing a virtual ball to one another. After a while, the virtual players would play only with each other. As the real subject realized he or she was being left out, brain scans revealed that the areas of the brain that were activated were the same as those sensing physical pain.[1] It really hurt! Such is the pain that charlatans use to manipulate others to their own advantage. Wanting to avoid it, we adapt and try to fit in.

Our ability to fit in depends on how well we understand the prevailing culture, adapt to the group's rules, and adopt that way of keeping score. While there are great variations in the norms, there are two basic patterns: Some cultures emphasize our need to connect, collaborate, and form lasting relationships, while others stress our need to acquire, compete, and do better than others.

Traditional cultures tend to favor relationships more than achievements. Such cultures are aligned with the Japanese saying, "The nail that sticks out quickly gets hammered down." Most of us who were raised in small towns know this way of life. In my native village in northern Denmark, respect was not measured in money; it was earned through hard work, integrity, and loyalty. Humility was a virtue, and we took pride in being modest. If you strayed, someone would quickly corral you and put you back in your place. Roles were not connected to competencies but to duties.

By contrast, modern, big-city cultures tend to favor getting ahead. When I worked in Los Angeles, personal bonds were temporary, and acquisition was the name of the game. "Get your name in lights," I was told; "you are what you drive," "loser is a four-letter word," and "the one with the most toys wins." This acquisition game dominates U.S. culture. To fit in, today's teens and adults want their personal space, television, cell phone, car, computer, and credit cards. We also expect choices, whether buying technology, sneakers, or vacations, or choosing a neighborhood, college, or doctor. We want an ever-greater standard of living, and we want it *now*! If we can't afford it, charge it! Henry Ford, the father of consumerism, would have been ecstatic.

HAVING A GOOD TIME

The great city where the Emperor lived was very enjoyable.
Every day many visitors came. . . .

The tale takes place in a happy, Disney-like, make-believe little land. The Emperor dresses up, is surrounded by smiling "cast members," and everyone lines up and cheers at the processions. Fitting in is playful, lighthearted, and fun.

As in the tale, we also know how to have fun. In our youth, we were part of sets or cliques, where our only purpose was to hang out and have a good time. We enjoyed good music and good friends. Life was a beach!

As we grow older, however, the practical reasons for fitting in take over and we forget the lightheartedness. Family dinners become something we squeeze in. Kidding around with colleagues is dropped because of deadlines. Friends fall by the wayside.

Maybe we can learn something from the characters in the tale. Even though fitting in makes them foolish, they do remember to have fun.

PLAYING OUR ROLE

No one would let it be noticed that he could not see anything,
for then he would have been unfit for his position or very stupid.

All of us have a face we show to the world, a closely shaved or nicely made-up face, a company face. When we put on this face we get ready to perform, to say and do the things that fit our image and help us fit in. We know how to play the part of an enthusiastic supporter even when we cannot see "the cloth." We perform as expected.[2]

Playing different roles makes life interesting. I remember eating lunch with a group of Canadian police officers during a leadership program and being surprised when one of the men said that he played the "bad cop" during interrogations. I knew that in his job he investigated many child abuse cases, but he was also a very caring and empathic man, so I would surely have pegged him for the "good cop." Because I looked incredulous, he gave me a quick demonstration. Clearly he knew the role and performed it with passion.

Playing a role is all right. But when we give the same performance day after day, month after month, and year after year, we sometimes *become* the role. Sitting in a café I overheard a British man giving a friend an update about his three sons. Apparently, Michael was still very nice, but the two others had become rather edgy. He explained, "You know, they work in the City." It seemed the investment-banker behaviors that helped them succeed at work were creating problems at home.

Sometimes the role not only spills over, it takes over and becomes our main source of identity. A friend of mine, then a vice president of human resources, told me of a conversation with another corporate VP. This man had lamented how, after being let go from his previous firm, he was no longer invited to the events he had been included in before. He felt hurt. My friend, a rather plain-spoken woman, responded, "Why be hurt? Those people were never inviting *you* in the first place; they were always inviting your title." She thought it was plain foolish to confuse who we are, our deepest essence, with the positions we hold and the roles we play.

Behind the roles we perform is our private self—our personal thoughts, feelings, deliberations, and decisions. We could call this our "personal manager." When this part of us is well developed, we have good self-control, make good decisions, and have the discipline to see them through. For example, we may sit in a meeting where everyone, including our boss, raves about a business guru's latest book. How should we act if we think the book "doesn't have anything on"? Should we ask "dumb" questions? Should we speak our mind, fake it, or be quiet? What might be the consequences of our decision? Working behind the scenes, a competent "personal manager" will make the best call. In the tale, we can observe the personal manager at work when the trusted minister and then another official were sent to see how the cloth was coming along. When they did not see it, we can hear their personal managers, first wondering whether they are stupid or incompetent, then quickly deciding to play it safe. By choosing safety over honesty, they ended up doing a poor job in their roles as trusted advisers. This episode rings true because many of us have faced similar dilemmas and rationalized our decisions as "practical."

Obviously we need to keep an eye on our personal manager's tendency to be overly practical. Sometimes, as in the tale, it may come as a response to a current situation. Other times, however, that practicality is more strategic, as when we constantly look for ways to build a better resume and package ourselves for corporate consumption. This is fine, as long as we do not give up our dreams and longings in exchange. Sadly, however, people have often sacrificed what they loved for something that at the time seemed to make sense, only to find they had made a bad bargain.

In the 1980s, management careers seemed like a safe bet until reengineering "cut out the fat." In the 1990s, the computer field promised a golden future, yet it did not take long for premium jobs to move overseas. If we sacrifice what we love for an uncertain future, we are probably making a bad decision. Often the most practical thing we can do is to spend less time strategizing and planning for an unpredictable future and more time paying attention to our passion and potential. Only then are we likely to both be employable and find satisfaction in our work.

PLAYING IT SAFE

"It is magnifique! *Exquisite! Excellent!"*

We do many things to fit in, from showing good manners to meeting deadlines, and there is nothing wrong with that. The problem occurs when, in order to fit in, we disregard the facts and act contrary to our own values. Then, seeking to fit in becomes foolish. Why do we do it? Often it is a matter of fear, of playing it safe. We want to look smart, avoid "career-limiting moves," and keep our jobs.

The fear is often caused by financial vulnerabilities. When we are over our ears in debt or the job market is soft, we feel exposed and we play it safe. We accept the opinions of dominant players and deny our own—we adopt their agenda. In the tale the characters cannot see the new clothes, but because they fear rejection, they disregard their own experience and say the expected.

In today's workplace we deal with similar vulnerabilities. If we let on that we cannot see that the new strategy is brilliant, we could be considered "impermissibly stupid." If we do not applaud the new products or cheer the restructuring, we could be judged as "unfit for our position." So, we publicly say the right words, even when we privately think something else. We feel at risk, so we play it safe. When teenagers go along, we say they give in to peer pressure. But when adults do it, we say we are practical.

We go along because our boss and others higher in the hierarchy act as if they control our careers, and we buy into that view. We believe that as long as we play by their rules we will be rewarded; that as long as we hit the numbers on their scoreboard we will succeed. Then, when they cannot deliver, we feel cheated. We need to realize that their power is limited and trust our own.

We adapt because corporations have carefully constructed their images and we expect them to be stable and solid. Yet, frequent mergers, buy-outs, consolidations, and outsourcing make them unpredictable. As the "rulers" change, the rules are modified and the scoreboard adjusted. Our pet project is dropped, our "A" team is offshored, and our department is downsized; even then, we rationalize that at least we have health insurance. We must open our eyes. In the global economy, corporations will continue to change. We are free agents, and our only security is our talent and track record.

We comply because we like our standard of living. We worry that if we speak our mind, our career will screech to a halt and our lifestyle will be downsized. Most of us feel trapped by mortgage, car, tuition, and credit card payments. We give up our freedom to pay for our way of life.

Pam Walsh, a mid-life career coach, finds that debt undermines courage. She has her clients build a Freedom Fund. This can be done in small ways by, for example, returning impulse purchases and depositing the refund into a special account. For a friend of mine, who is extremely fond of new clothes and accessories, that approach has created a nice cushion in just three years. More drastic steps could be to sell that third car or move into a smaller house.

When we face our fears and deal with them, we are able to resist "peer pressure" and also be practical.

KEEPING OUR EGOS IN CHECK

The Emperor had an outfit for every hour of the day . . .

The main point of *The Emperor's New Clothes* is that fitting in can also be foolish. Very often, what makes us act foolishly is our ego. When our ego gets inflated we buy our own press and disregard the facts, or we get enamored with our own ideas and stop listening to others. Ego, in the form of vanity, can make us trust a clever sales pitch more than our own reason.

In the tale, the Emperor is vanity personified. He was so exceedingly fond of beautiful new clothes that he spent all his money on being properly dressed, a clear sign of an ego out of control. Certainly, enjoying life's finer things can be fun, but to spend all of one's money on finery is rather foolish.

Great leaders know how to keep their egos in check and avoid such silliness. They have a few trusted advisers, encourage dissent, and listen. Likewise, H. C. Andersen had close friends who were blunt with their feedback. Without them, much of his writing might have been trite and romantic (as some of it was), instead of insightful and enduring.

Each of us needs a few people who will level with us, whether they are friends, family, colleagues, or a coach. We do not always need to take their advice, but we do need to pay attention—particularly when we notice a pattern. Recently, while staying with the Spanish side of my family in a mountain village, I excused myself from a night of drinking and dancing at the village festival. I said to my brother-in-law, "I'm just really busy with the book right now," and his casual response was "You're always busy." For some reason I was bothered by his comment. Certainly my Spanish and Danish relatives had mentioned before that I was becoming too "American" in my intensity and drive and that I needed to make more time for relaxation and celebration. In the past I had brushed off similar comments, but this time it got to me. I love my work, but was it becoming an obsession instead of a passion? Was I unthinkingly replacing one exciting project with the next? Is work my vanity? I am still pondering that.

What are your vanities? What makes you feel attractive, smart, or important? Is it being on the "A" team, being consulted by someone important, making a lot of money, looking young? If so, what are the consequences? Is the game bringing you alive, or is it killing you? Such questions increase our self-awareness, which ultimately is our best defense against such foolishness.

MY OWN FOOLISHNESS

In the early 1980s I acted as foolishly as the characters in this tale. Because of fear and ego, I ignored my own judgment and complied.

At the time, women were not considered assertive enough to be managers or rational enough to be executives. We did not fit in. So, as the first woman manager in a multinational manufacturing firm, I worked hard, acted tough, and laughed at the sexist jokes. I was soon rewarded with a prestigious line-leader position.

One day my boss and boss's boss asked me to implement a plan that I thought would mislead the customers. I naively raised the question of ethics and instantly realized my mistake. The two men exchanged a look that said, "I knew we should never have hired a girl." They then made it clear that if I could not handle my responsibilities, they would find a man for the job. Hearing the brakes slam on my career, I assured them I would take care of it right away.

I rationalized my lack of courage by reminding myself of the hefty mortgage for my hillside home. Who could argue with being financially responsible? Also, transitioning from the public sector into business, I was new to the for-profit game. In addition, having come from an all-women physical therapy department, I thought that if I wanted to play with the boys, I had to play by their rules. It was a very logical decision, but I did not feel good about it. Deep inside, I was disappointed in the woman I was becoming.

Over time, my essential self began to assert itself. Why had I adopted such an expensive lifestyle in the first place? Was it bringing me alive or was it killing me? Also, had my ego not spun out of control? To be honest, did I not take pride in being the fast-track, golden girl? Did I not relish my full-page picture in the annual report, my big budget, and my high-visibility position?

When I finally opened my eyes, I realized that my debts had made me lose courage. So my husband and I simplified our life to the point that we could live on one income. This has given us the freedom to speak our minds (not that we do so gratuitously) and to make unconventional career moves. We traded a comfortable standard of living for a better quality of life.

FACING FACTS

"But he doesn't have anything on," said a little child. . . . "He doesn't have anything on!" everyone finally shouted.

When H. C. Andersen first sent the manuscript for *The Emperor's New Clothes* to his publisher, he maintained the illusion till the very end. The original closing lines were: "'I must certainly put on these robes every time I walk in a procession or appear before an assembly' said the Emperor, and the whole town talked about his wonderful new clothes."

Thus the ego was stroked, roles were maintained, and people had a good time. Yet, they had been manipulated, cheated, and left doubting their own judgment.

Fortunately, before the pamphlet went to print, H. C. Andersen changed the ending by adding the child's guileless observation, "But he doesn't have anything on." That made the ending less cynical and more ambiguous.

When faced with the truth, does the Emperor ignore or accept it? I used to think he remained in denial, because the text says, "And the Emperor shuddered, for it seemed to him that they were right." The word *seemed* led me to believe he did not face facts. Also, if he admits he has been cheated, why does he not set out to catch the charlatans? (See the "Did You Know . . ." section above.) But could the ending be interpreted in a more positive way?

A friend of mine, an experienced children's book editor and H. C. Andersen aficionada, believes the ending is hopeful. She believes the Emperor, at the most humiliating moment of his life, finally steps up to his responsibility. Here is a man whose identity is to be well dressed now stripped of his finery, stark naked, and exposed as a fool. Yet, he does not fall apart. He lifts his head, squares his shoulders, and sees the procession through. In her opinion, where previously he was just dressing up as an Emperor, he finally has the courage to act like one.

My friend's interpretation is aligned with what we know about addictive behaviors. The end of the line for alcoholics is often some final and complete humiliation, which forces them to open their eyes. Facing the facts, they are able to stand up at an AA (Alcoholics Anonymous) meeting and say the words, "My name is [first name], and I'm an alcoholic." Stripped naked, all illusions gone, they are ready to begin the tough journey to sobriety.

Facing facts is important not only for individuals but also for high-performing teams. Working adults who have the ability to be frank and descriptive are a great asset to their teams; that is, if finger pointing is avoided and the team wants to be great.

The child's statement "But he doesn't have anything on!" is an example of how to speak candidly. Because the statement is self-evident, people readily agree. Had the child thrown about opinions, such as "the Emperor is a fool," others would have disagreed. They might have argued, "No, the Emperor is naive," or "No, the Emperor needs to be more careful picking his advisers."

Unfortunately, instead of being descriptive, teams often want to rehash old resentments and reveal other people's shortcomings, even though such grumbling is useless. In my engagements with leadership teams, we inevitably do our best work when we are genuinely curious about the mess we are in (for example, being unprepared for a tremendous opportunity), candid and clear about what caused it, and able to own up to and even laugh at our foolishness.* Then the journey of becoming a stronger team can begin. Letting go of illusions about oneself, the team, or the company is tough, but it is part of growing up.

*If you would like a complimentary copy of "Guidelines for Candid Team Conversations," please go to www.mettenorgaard.com.

WHOSE AGENDA ARE YOU ON?

Ultimately, one of the main lessons of this tale is that we must look at whether we are in control of our own agenda. When we are anxious to fit in, we live our lives on other people's agenda. This may have advantages in the short term but is very risky in the long term. When we become too practical and calculating about our careers, we tightly manage them to fit other people's expectations. We choose the profession other people suggest, learn the competencies they require, and respond to their semi-annual performance reviews. We listen to what our boss, human resources, and other key players have to say. We give up our desires, adapt to their rules, and adopt their scoreboard. Then later, if our jobs become downsized, outsourced, or offshored, we feel betrayed.

We can do better than that by reclaiming our own agenda, by choosing the work we feel passionate about, the work that we can do better than anyone else. As a result, instead of feeling entitled, we become responsible. Most important, we become world-class at what we do and enjoy the process.

When our self-esteem depends on the approval of others and on the perks or promotions they can give or withhold, *they* are in control. We can reclaim our own agenda by using two terrific "fool detectors"—our self-awareness to guide us from the inside, and candid conversations to prod us from the outside. Both are activated by the question "Whose agenda am I on?" If we are on other people's agenda, we need to stop and examine the situation. As we counterbalance our practical personality with our deeper interests, as we honestly look at our fears and ego, we become immune to manipulation.

The Emperor's New Clothes helps us chuckle at life's difficult moments and our own silliness. H. C. Andersen's intent with this tale is not to judge us, but to ask us to be authentic. He does not denigrate us, but he does ask us to be aware. He invites us to have some fun but not be foolish.

SOMETHING TO THINK ABOUT...

Are you running on the ever-greater-standard-of-living treadmill? If so, is it energizing you or is it killing you?

What makes you choose to speak up? What makes you say the expected or stay quiet?

SOMETHING TO TALK TO YOUR COLLEAGUES ABOUT...

At work, what things cannot be discussed? How do you know?

Who on the team is able to raise tough issues? How do they do that?

2

THE UGLY DUCKLING

■

When we heed our longing,
we grow into our "swanlike" nature.

■

"IT WAS SO LOVELY out in the country. It was summer! The wheat stood yellow, the oats green, and the hay was stacked down in the green meadow." *The Ugly Duckling* thus begins in a lovely pastoral setting and finishes in an even more idyllic garden. But separating the two peaceful scenes is a fierce tale of rejection, survival, longing, learning, and growing into the person we were meant to be.

The theme is the timeless and universal story of the hero's journey. The ugly duckling has a wretched childhood. He is so dejected throughout the tale that it is wonderfully surprising when he finally shows some backbone. First his survival instincts kick in, and he says "no" to abuse. Then his identity asserts itself, and he says "no" to conformity. Finally his "swan-like" nature, his essence, is expressed as he says "yes" to his potential.

As you read the following summary or, if you prefer, the full tale, consider these questions: What inspires you about the story? What do you find disheartening? What do you long for?

A SUMMARY OF THE TALE

One summer, close to the moat of a manor house, a mother duck was nesting. One by one the eggs cracked, but an uncommonly large one remained. An old duck insisted it was a turkey egg and warned the mother that turkeys were afraid of water. When it finally cracked, a large, ugly duckling tumbled out. Fearing he was indeed a turkey, the mother thought, "Into the water with him, even if I have to kick him in."

She brought her brood down to the moat, and one after the other the ducklings plopped in and they all floated splendidly, including the ugly one. "No, that's no turkey!" thought the mother, "He's my own all right!"

Once in the duck yard, the others picked on the ugly one for he was so different. The ducks bit him, the hens pecked him, and even the girl who came to feed them kicked him. His sisters and brothers said they hoped the cat would take him, and eventually even the mother wished him far away. In desperation, the duckling fled over the fence and escaped to the marshland.

In the wilderness he met some friendly wild geese. But suddenly a hunt was on! The geese were shot, the water turned red with blood, and a fearsome dog came splashing and retrieved the dead geese. The duckling was absolutely terrified.

At night, the duckling fled the marsh and came to a dilapidated farmhouse where an old woman lived with her cat and hen.

The cat was the master of the house, the hen the missus, and both were full of opinions. The duckling thought one could have a different point of view, but they would not stand for it. Though safe in his corner, the duckling began to long for the outdoors and the water and confided in the hen. But she insisted that it was idleness that gave him such silly notions and told him to get busy. When the longing persisted, the hen told the duckling he was unreasonable. Did he think the cat, the hen, or the old woman wanted to splash around? His idea was pure nonsense! "But you don't understand me!" the duckling cried, and he went out into the wide world.

Back in his element, the duckling loved floating and diving, but the other creatures continued to reject him. One fall evening the duckling noticed a flock of beautiful white birds with long, graceful necks: They were swans! The majestic creatures spread their wings and flew away toward warmer climates. The duckling felt strangely connected. Although they soon disappeared from sight, there was no way he could forget those stunning creatures.

Winter came and the poor little duckling had to swim about to keep the water from freezing completely. But in the end he got tired and was trapped in the ice. Fortunately a farmer saw him and rescued him.

Finally spring returned and the duckling tested his wings. They made a strong swooshing sound as they carried him to a beautiful garden. When he landed on the water, he saw the majestic birds again, but this time they were coming toward him with their feathers all puffed up. He feared they might hack him to death for being so hideous. Accepting his fate, he bowed his head toward the surface of the still water and suddenly he saw his own reflection—he was himself a swan!

DID YOU KNOW . . . In November 1843

H. C. Andersen published a pamphlet of tales that included *The Ugly Duckling* and *The Nightingale*. For the first time the author deleted the words "told for children" from the pamphlet's title page, as he now saw himself as writing for both children *and* adults—the plot intended to entertain the child while the underlying ideas were meant to engage the adults. With this volume H. C. Andersen finally became a literary and commercial success.

The Ugly Duckling is the most autobiographical of his works, and scholars recognize every mood and feeling from his letters and journal entries. H. Topsøe-Jensen draws several parallels to the story, observing that the author, just like the duckling, was "the poor one, dependent on benefactors who did not understand him, tormented and mistreated, full of feelings of inferiority, enduring long and difficult times troubled by doubts about his own worth, but deep inside secretly convinced that 'the hour of reckoning' would come."[1]

Like the hero of this tale, H. C. Andersen had an inclination toward self-pity and self-dramatization, but he too was surprisingly courageous. These tendencies were understandable, for there was nothing romantic about H. C. Andersen's childhood. Not only was his family poor, but it was also less than respectable. His parents barely married before he was born, his grandmother had been jailed for having too many illegitimate children, his grandfather was in the lunatic asylum, and his illegitimate half-sister worked in a brothel. Furthermore, he was an effeminate and ugly boy, with feet that were too big, limbs that were too long, and eyes that were too small. Yet, through his own merit, H. C. Andersen made his way to Copenhagen, gained royal patronage, and became one of the best-loved authors in the world.

THE CLASSIC TALE

IT WAS SO LOVELY *out in the country. It was summer! The wheat stood yellow, the oats green, and the hay was stacked down in the green meadow. And there a stork walked on his long red legs, chattering in Egyptian, for that was the language he had learned from his mother. All around the fields and meadows were large forests, and in the middle of the forests were deep lakes. Yes, it was so very lovely out there in the country.*

The sun shone down on an old manor house with a deep moat all around it, and from the wall down to the water grew large-leaf weeds. They were so tall that little children could stand upright under the biggest ones. It was just as wild in there as in the thickest forest. And here sat a duck on her nest. She had to hatch her little ducklings, but she was getting tired of it, for it took a very long time and she seldom got any company. The other ducks liked swimming about in the moat more than running up and sitting under the weeds to chat with her.

Finally one egg after another stated cracking: "Peep! Peep!" All the egg yolks had come alive and a little head stuck out of each shell.

"Quack! Quack!" said the mother, and the ducklings then hurried as fast as they could, and looked all about under the green

leaves. The mother let them look as much as they wanted to, for green is good for the eyes.

"My, how big the world is!" said all the ducklings, for they certainly had a lot more room than when they were lying in the eggs.

"You think this is the whole world," said the mother, "but it reaches far beyond the garden, right to the minister's field, though I myself have never been there! Well, now I expect you're all here!"—and she got up.

"No, I don't have everyone! The biggest egg is still lying there. How long is this one going to take? I'm beginning to get bored with it!" And then she sat down again.

"Well, how's it going?" said an old duck that had come to pay a visit.

"It takes so long with this one egg!" said the duck that was sitting. "It won't crack. But do come and see the others! They're the loveliest ducklings I've ever seen. They all look like their father, that scoundrel; he doesn't come to see me."

"Let me see the egg that won't crack!" said the old one. "Believe me, that's a turkey egg! I was fooled that way once myself. And I had such grief and trouble with those youngsters for, I tell you, they're afraid of the water! I couldn't get them to go in! I quacked and snapped, but nothing helped. Let me see that egg! Yes, that's a turkey egg all right! You just leave that one and teach your other children to swim."

"Well, I'll sit on it a little longer," said the duck. "Now that I've sat here this long, I might as well sit it out!"

"Suit yourself!" said the old duck. And then she left.

Finally the large egg cracked. "Peep! Peep!" said the youngster as he tumbled out. He was big and ugly. The mother looked at him. "Now, that is one horribly big duckling!" she said. "None of the others looks like that! It couldn't be a turkey chick, could it? Well, we'll soon find out! Into the water with him, even if I have to kick him in!"

The next day the weather was glorious. The sun was shining on the green weeds. The mother duck with her whole family went down to the moat. Splash! She jumped into the water. "Quack. Quack!" she said, and one duckling after another plopped in. The water splashed over their heads, but they quickly came up again and floated along beautifully. Their legs worked all by themselves, so all of them were soon well out in the water, and even the ugly gray one was swimming along.

"No, that's no turkey!" she said. "Look how nicely he's using his legs, and how tall he carries himself. He's my own all right. Actually he's quite handsome when you really look at him. Quack. Quack. Now come along, and I'll take you out in the world and introduce you to the duck yard. But stay close to me so no one steps on you, and watch out for the cat!"

And then they came to the duck yard. There was a terrible ruckus in there, for there were two families fighting over an eel's head, which the cat got in the end.

"See, that's how the world is," said the duck mother and licked her bill, for she also wanted the eel's head. "Now use your legs!" she said. "Hurry up and bow to the old one over there! She's the most distinguished of everyone here. She has Spanish blood, that's why she's so fat. And notice, she has a red rag around her leg. That's something very special, and it's the greatest honor anyone can receive. It is so important that no one would want to get rid of her, and it means that she'll be recognized by animals and humans! Now hurry along! Don't keep your legs together! A properly brought-up duckling sets its legs wide apart, just like its father and mother. That's it! Now bow with your neck and say 'Quack!'"

And so they did, but the other ducks around them looked at them and said quite loudly, "Look at that! Now we're going to have another bunch! As if we weren't enough already! And yuck! How that one duckling looks! We won't put up with him!" And right away one duck flew over and bit him on the neck.

"Let him alone!" said the mother. "He's not bothering anyone!"

"Yes, but he's too big and peculiar," said the duck that had bit him, "and so he has to get picked on!"

"Those are pretty children the mother has!" said the old duck with the rag around her leg. "All of them are pretty except one; that one did not turn out well. I wish she could do that one over again."

"That's not possible, your grace," said the mother duck. "He's not pretty, but he has a really good nature, and he swims as well as the others! Yes, I dare say, even a little better! I think he'll grow handsome, or that in time he will become a little smaller. He's been too long in the egg, that's why he hasn't got the right shape." And then she nuzzled his neck and smoothed his feathers. "Besides, he's only a drake," she said, "and so it doesn't matter so much. I think he'll become very strong. He'll make it, all right."

"The other ducklings are lovely," said the old one. "Just make yourselves at home, and if you find an eel's head, you may bring it to me."

And so they made themselves at home.

But the poor duckling, who had been the last one out of the egg, and who was so ugly, was bitten, shoved, and made fun of, and that by both the ducks and the hens. "He's too big!" they all said. And the turkey rooster, who had been born with spurs and therefore thought he was an emperor, puffed himself up like a ship at full sail. He went straight at the duckling, and then he gobbled and turned quite red in the face. The poor duckling didn't know whether he dared stay or leave. He was miserable because he felt monstrous and was mocked by the whole duck yard.

That's how it went the first day, and after that it got worse and worse. The poor duckling was chased by all of them; even his brothers and sisters were mean to him, and they always said: "If only the cat would get you, you horrid monster!" And his mother said, "If only you were far away!" The ducks bit him, the hens pecked him, and the girl who fed the animals kicked him.

Finally, he ran and flew over the fence, and the little birds in the bushes were startled and flew up. "It's because I'm so hideous," thought the duckling, and shut his eyes, but he still kept on running. Then he came to the large marsh where the wild ducks lived. He lay there the whole night; he was so tired and unhappy.

In the morning some wild ducks flew up and took a look at their new buddy. "What sort of creature are you?" they asked, and the duckling turned to all sides and greeted them as best he could.

"You're really ugly," said the wild ducks. "But that doesn't matter to us as long as you don't marry into our family!" Poor thing! The duckling certainly wasn't thinking about getting married; he scarcely dared to lie in the rushes and drink a little marsh water.

There he lay two whole days. Then came two wild geese, or rather wild ganders, for they were two males. It had not been long since they had come out of the egg, and so they were quite lively.

"Listen, buddy," they said, "you're so ugly that I like you! Do you want to come along and be a migratory bird? Close by in another marsh are some sweet and beautiful wild geese, all of them maidens who can say 'Quack!' You might get lucky, as ugly as you are!"

Bang! Bang! it sounded at that moment right above them. Then both wild ganders fell down dead in the rushes, and the water turned red as blood. Bang! Bang! it sounded again, and whole flocks of wild geese flew up out of the rushes, and then there were more shots. It was a great hunt. The hunters lay in different places in the marsh. Yes, some even sat up on the tree branches that reached far out over the rushes. The blue smoke drifted like clouds through the dark trees and hung far out over the water. The hunting dogs came through the mud, splash, splash, and the rushes and reeds swayed back and forth. It was terrifying for the poor little duckling. He turned his head to tuck it under his wing, and, just then, a terribly big dog appeared in front of him. Its tongue was hanging way out of its mouth, and its eyes were glinting horribly. Its open jaws bore down upon the duckling, sharp teeth bared, and—splash! splash!—it ran off without taking him.

"Oh, dear God," sighed the duckling, "I'm so disgusting that even the dog doesn't feel like biting me!" Then he lay quite still while buckshot whistled through the rushes, as shot after shot rang out.

It didn't get quiet until late in the day, but still the poor duckling dared not get up. He waited several more hours before he looked around, and then he hurried from the marsh as fast as he could, running across fields and meadows. It was so windy that he had a hard time moving.

Toward evening he reached a sad little farmhouse. It was so dilapidated that it did not know to which side it was going to fall, so it remained standing. The wind whooshed so hard around the duckling that he had to sit down on his bottom to stay put. And it got worse and worse. Then he noticed that the door had come off one of its hinges and hung so crookedly that he could slip into the living room through the opening, and he did.

There lived an old woman with her cat and her hen. The cat, whom she called Sonny, could arch his back and purr. He even threw off sparks, but for that one had to stroke him the wrong way. The hen had very short, low legs, so she was called Chickedy-Low-Legs. She laid many eggs, and the old woman was as fond of her as if she were her own child.

In the morning they noticed the stranger right away, and the cat began to purr and the hen to cluck.

"What's this?" said the woman, looking around. She didn't see so well, so she thought that the duckling was a fat duck that had gotten lost. "Well, that's a nice catch!" she said. "Now I can have duck eggs, if only it isn't a male duck. But we have to try!"

So the duckling was accepted on trial for three weeks, but there were no eggs. The cat was the master of the house, and the hen was the missus. They always said, "We and the world!" for they believed that they were half of the world—what is more, the very best half. The duckling thought that one could have a different opinion, but the hen would not stand for it.

"Can you lay eggs?" she asked.

"No!"

"Then, you'd better keep your mouth shut!"

And the cat said, "Can you arch your back, purr, and throw off sparks?"

"No!"

"Then you should keep your opinions to yourself when sensible folks are talking!"

The duckling sat in the corner and was in a bad mood. He began to think about the fresh air and the sunshine, and then he had a very strange desire to float on the water. In the end he couldn't help himself, and he had to tell the hen about it.

"What's the matter with you?" she asked. "You have nothing to do, that's it! That's why you're getting these strange ideas. Lay eggs or purr, then it will pass."

"But it's so wonderful to float on the water," said the duckling, "so lovely to get it over your head and dive down to the bottom!"

"Well, what a great pleasure that would be," said the hen. "You must have gone mad! Just ask the cat, he's the wisest I know, whether he likes to float on water or dive down! I won't even speak of myself. You can even ask our mistress, the old woman, no one in the world is wiser than she is. Do you think she feels like floating and getting water over her head?"

"You don't understand me," said the duckling.

"Well, if we don't understand you, who would? You're not thinking that you're wiser than the cat and the old woman, not to mention myself! Don't make a fuss, child! And thank your creator for all the good we have done for you. Haven't you come into a warm room and been able to be around people you could learn something from? Yet you're a fool, and it's no fun being around you! Believe me, it's for your own good that I tell you the harsh truth, and that's the way one can know one's true friends! Now you just get started laying eggs or learn how to purr or throw off sparks!"

"I think I'll go out into the wide world," said the duckling.

"Yes, you do that," said the hen.

So the duckling went out into the wide world and floated on the water and dived down. But all the other animals still ignored him because of his ugliness.

Autumn came. The leaves in the wood turned gold and brown, and the wind grabbed hold of them so they danced about. The air looked cold, and the clouds hung heavy with hail and snow. A raven sat on the fence and cried "Ow! Ow!" from sheer cold. Yes, one could really freeze at the thought of it. The poor little duckling most definitely did not feel good.

One evening, as the sun was setting so gloriously, a large flock of beautiful big birds came out of the bushes. The duckling had never seen anything so lovely. They were gleaming white with long graceful necks; they were swans! They uttered a strange cry and spread their magnificent great wings to fly away from the cold regions to warmer lands and unfrozen lakes. They rose higher and higher, and the little duckling felt most strange. He circled around in the water, and stretched his neck high up in the air toward them and suddenly let out a cry so loud and so strange that he even frightened himself.

Oh, he could not forget those beautiful birds, those happy birds. When he could no longer see them, he dove down to the bottom, and when he came up again, he was beside himself. He didn't know what those birds were called or where they flew off to, but even so he loved them—loved them more than he had ever loved anyone. He was not envious, for it never occurred to him to wish for such loveliness for himself. He would have been happy if the ducks had just tolerated him, poor ugly creature that he was.

The winter was cold, so very cold. The duckling had to swim about continuously to keep the swimming hole from freezing completely, but each night the hole became smaller and smaller. The frost was so deep that the ice groaned. The duckling had to move his legs all the time to keep the hole from freezing over. In the end he became so weak he lay quite still, and then he froze fast in the ice.

Early in the morning a farmer came by. He saw the duckling, went out and broke the ice with his wooden shoe, and then carried him home to his wife. There he was brought back to life.

The children wanted to play with him, but the duckling thought they wanted to hurt him, and, being scared, he rushed up into the milk pan so the milk splashed out in the room. The wife shrieked and waved her arms in the air. Then he flew into the trough with the butter and then down into the flour barrel and up again. What a sight he was! The wife screamed and tried to hit him with the fire tongs, and the children stumbled over each other trying to catch the duckling as they laughed and screamed. It was a good thing that the door was open, and the duckling was able to rush out between the bushes that were covered with the newly fallen snow. And there he lay, as if hibernating.

It would be far too depressing to tell about all the danger and despair that he had to go through during the harsh winter. He was lying in the marsh among the rushes when the sun began to shine warmly and the skylarks began to sing. It was spring again!

Then all at once he lifted his wings. They swooshed stronger than before and powerfully carried him up and away. Before he knew it, he found himself in a large garden where apple trees blossomed and where the lilacs scented the air and hung on the long green branches all the way down to the winding canals. Oh, it was so lovely here, as fresh as spring! And straight ahead, out of the thicket came three beautiful white swans; they puffed up their feathers and floated ever so lightly on the water! The duckling recognized the beautiful birds and was overcome with a strange sadness.

"I will fly over to them, those regal birds! Though they will bite me to death because I dare to approach them, I who am so repulsive. But it doesn't matter. Better be killed by them than be bitten by the ducks, pecked by the hens, kicked by the girl who takes care of the chicken yard, and suffer through another winter!" And he flew out into the water and swam toward the magnificent swans. They saw him and, with puffed-up feathers, they rushed toward him. "Go ahead, kill me," said the poor creature, as he bowed his head down toward the surface of the water awaiting his death—but what did he see in the clear water? He saw his own reflection. He was no longer a clumsy, black-gray bird, ugly and disgusting. He was himself a swan!

It doesn't matter if you are born in a duck yard, as long as you come from a swan's egg.

He then felt really happy about all the suffering and adversity that he had gone through, because now he truly appreciated his good fortune and all the loveliness that awaited him. The large swans swam around him and stroked him with their bills.

Some small children came into the garden. They threw bread and grain out into the water, and the smallest one yelled: "There's a new one!" And all the children shouted with joy, saying, "Yes, a new one has arrived!" They clapped their hands and danced around and ran to get their father and mother. Then they threw bread and cake into the water, and they all said, "The new one is the most beautiful! So young and lovely!" And the old swans bowed to him.

Then he felt quite shy and put his head under his wing—he did not know what to do. He was much too happy! But he was not proud, for a good heart is never proud! He thought about how he had been mistreated and mocked, and now he heard everyone say that he was the loveliest of all the lovely birds. The lilacs bowed to him, lowering their branches all the way down to the water, and the sun shone so warm and bright. And then he puffed up his feathers, lifted his slender neck, and rejoiced with all his heart: "I never dreamt there could be so much happiness when I was the ugly duckling."

THE TALE AT WORK

We do not succeed in life by having an enviable career; we succeed by finding where we belong and becoming the person we were meant to be. Just because we live and work with certain people, that does not mean we belong with them; we belong with those who share or encourage our longing. Also, just because we grow older, that does not mean we grow into who we were meant to be. We grow into our essence only when our false self-images die and our true self is born.

The journey of self-discovery is inconvenient. It takes us from periods of stability and integration to instability and intense growth, back to stability and integration at the next level. When two-year olds or teenagers move through instability, we consider it normal and say they are being "difficult"; but when adults do it, we think it is self-indulgent and say they are irresponsible. Yet, only by questioning conformity and ruffling a few feathers can we grow into a greater view of ourselves, our work, and the world.

A GREATER VIEW OF SELF

The ugly duckling does not fit in. He is mobbed for being too different, too big, and too ugly. Similarly, many in the workplace feel discriminated against for not fitting the mold, whether because of gender, race, religion, education, or temperament. While such judgments can be hurtful, the serious damage occurs only if we adopt other people's opinions as our own.

Leaving Negative Voices Behind

Not surprisingly, the ugly duckling develops a pitiful self-image. When a flock of birds are surprised, he thinks they fly up because he is hideous, and when a hunting dog doesn't retrieve him, he reasons, "I'm so disgusting that even the dog doesn't feel like biting me." Like the duckling, many of us have a harsh inner critic who constantly reminds us of our shortcomings and undermines our self-esteem. Others have the opposite problem and need to prop up their over-inflated sense of self with inner pep talks. Either way, such self-talk keeps us from connecting to our essential nature. We need to leave these false voices behind before we can hear our own true voice.

Asserting Oneself

After escaping the abuse in the duck yard and the violence in the marsh, the duckling finds safety with the old woman and her cat and hen. Unlike the mother duck, who simply conforms, the cat and the hen want control. They regularly preface their statements with, "We and the world!" as they think they are half of the world, and "what is more, the very best half." They are like managers who see themselves as the brains of the company, and the best brains at that, or like recalcitrant coworkers who feel superior to management as they resist every change.

Stuck in a corner, the duckling begins to long for the water, wishing he could splash it over his head and dive way down to the bottom. The hen thinks his nonsensical yearning is caused by idleness and tells him to get busy. Fortunately, the duckling disregards the hen's advice and decides to follow his longing.

Most of us have a bossy hen in our life. We can easily spot her in a parent, an in-law, a spouse, friend, colleague, or manager, but we often fail to hear her clucking away in our own heads. She is the responsible, close-to-the-ground voice that squawks: "You can't pay attention to your longing right now; it would hurt your career." "You can't, you don't have the time." "You can't, others are counting on you."

Though her no-nonsense attitude helps us handle practical matters, we cannot let her run our life. If we do, we will become too busy to think and too closed-minded to learn, and we will grow old before our time.

Eleanor Roosevelt, America's First Lady from 1933 to 1945, characterized herself as an ugly duckling child. Orphaned at ten and brought up by relatives, she felt chronically inferior and fearful. Women of her generation were raised to serve their husbands, and she accepted that as her destiny. In addition she was faced with a domineering "hen" of a mother-in-law, and it took years before the young Eleanor dared to speak her mind even within her own family. But after two critical events—her husband's infidelity and then his polio—she began to stand her own ground. By the time she became First Lady, during the Great Depression and World War II, she was ready to go out into the wide world. She traveled the country and listened to those who were marginalized, those who had no voice. Plain looking and plain spoken, she became an advocate for those who were not allowed to speak for themselves, particularly women and African Americans. As she grew into her swanlike stature, she became one of the most admired Americans of her time.

In the fall, the duckling gets a glimpse of what he may become as he sees a flock of magnificent swans fly up and begin their migration. The vision of the birds is unsettling, yet also compelling, and it sustains him through the harsh winter.

In the spring, the fully grown duckling flies with powerful, swooshing strokes to a beautiful garden. There white swans rush toward him with their feathers all puffed up; destiny is moving in. Terrified, the duckling bows his head toward the clear water, where he finally sees his true image: He is himself a swan. This is the moment of transformation, as his false identity dies and the true one is born.

Approaching one's greatness can be terrifying. While we feel safe viewing something extraordinary from afar, we get frightened when it comes straight toward us and says, "Join us!" We fear that we will not measure up, that we will embarrass ourselves. We would rather not take the risk, so we pull back. Yet, only when we dare to engage with those we consider "great" may we see our true essence.

The ugly duckling's identity develops through the tale, and, similarly, each of us has our own inner journey to make. Do you sometimes look around and think, "I don't belong here"? Do you hold your own with opinionated hens? To whom are you drawn, with whom would you like to spend time, from whom would you love to learn?

A GREATER VIEW OF WORK

"But it's so wonderful to float on the water!" said the duckling, "so lovely to get it over your head and dive down to the bottom!"

Much of our identity and self-esteem is shaped by what we do. This was not always so. In H. C. Andersen's time it was your birth that dictated where you could live, the type of work you could do, and whom you could marry. I encountered remnants of this mindset when my husband and I spent last summer in a medieval mountain village in Spain. There the first question was "Who do you belong to?" and my identity was being the wife of Agustín's son, and Agustín was the former schoolmaster's son. After I returned to the United States, I went to a retreat, yet even in this contemplative setting, the first question was, "What do you do?" Work was our way to quickly tag one another. The contrast was startling, and it reminded me that in a merit-based society, work is a critical part of our identity. To paraphrase Descartes we might say, "I work therefore I am."

At times we thrive in our work, we love what we do, and we appreciate the people we work with. We are content. But inevitably something disturbs the peace. It may be external events such as a new boss, a new strategy, or a large-scale reorganization. Other times the changes may be internal. Maybe we feel a growing conflict between what we are asked to do and what we believe, maybe our heart is no longer in it, maybe we hear ourselves talking more about what is wrong than about what we love, maybe at the end of the day we feel drained, frustrated, crabby, restless, unfocused, or unsettled with life. We feel much like the duckling when he is stuck indoors. Yet, we often ignore the symptoms. We hope that if we just hang in there a little longer or try a little harder, things will get back to normal.

Sometimes we worry that "going out into the wide world" means that we have to quit our job and do something spectacular. But venturing forth is less about changing our jobs and more about changing ourselves. Jonathan Young, a former collaborator of the mythologist Joseph Campbell, believes that leaving one's job is often the easy way out. In a recent e-mail he wrote, "Deciding to stay in a job and finding a way to breathe new life into it is sometimes just as heroic and astoundingly creative as leaving."

The workers at the Pike Place Fish Market in Seattle are a great example of what Jonathan Young means. Being a fishmonger has never been among the top ten career choices for most people. The work is heavy, smelly, slimy, and slippery. Even so, the fishmongers at Pike Place take pride in their work, as shown in the documentary film *Fish*.

It all started with a boss who began to see his employees as having interests of their own and asked, "What can we do to create a better workplace?" One of the young fishmongers said, "As long as we're going to be spending all of our time here anyway, why don't we be world famous?"[2] At first the others dismissed his suggestion, but little by little the group began to talk about how they would treat one another if they were world famous fishmongers. They talked about how they would treat their customers. As they continued to talk about how they would act if they *were* world famous, they *became* world famous.

Today these fishmongers create an experience of such extraordinary service and of so much fun that the market has become one of Seattle's top tourist attractions. The change even paid off from a business perspective; what used to be a good week's revenue is now generated by Monday noon, without any increase in space or staff. These fishmongers show us that, by changing ourselves, we can indeed breathe new life into our work.

While I admire people like the fishmongers, my own career pattern shows that I tend to take the easy way out and leave. Being restless and bothered by "the toothache of the heart," I was always ready to go out into the wide world. Only, unlike the duckling, I did not know where I was going. In my first career as a physical therapist, I remember feeling I did not belong and talked to a colleague about wanting to do something worthwhile.

She said, "Mette, you make lame people walk! How much more meaningful do you need your work to be?" She was right that physical therapy was *good* work; it just was not *my* work. Several detours later, I finally realized that *my* work was to help others draw on their essential nature to give a great performance, to help them be alive in their work.

Having overdosed on self-help books, I was slow to pick up Stephen R. Covey's book, *The Seven Habits of Highly Effective People*. But when I finally read it, I discovered a framework for personal development that was inspirational, substantive, and practical. I became so excited that I joined The Covey Leadership Center and found myself swimming with hundreds of swans that shared my passion for leadership. The power and swoosh of our wings when we took off was an incredible rush! But, as always, things changed. In this case, the company faced changes in market conditions and customer expectations and responded with a merger, new leadership, new strategies, and new content. Over time, the firm's interests and mine diverged, and I needed to leave the idyllic garden to create my own content. Still, I treasure the memory of swimming with swans.

Whether we help re-create our current workplace or we leave, becoming more authentic is never easy. When Joseph Campbell said, "follow your bliss" he did not mean, "go have a good time." He was saying, "pay attention to the small, still voice—to that unique calling that seems to know your name."[3] Doing that will always be risky, for that whisper will not lead us along a predictable career path. Instead, it will ask us to make our own way.

When you are dissatisfied with work, do you tend to conform and complain and hope that things will get back to "normal"? Do you tend to become "astoundingly creative" with what you have? Do you literally go out into the wide world?

A GREATER VIEW OF THE WORLD

Then all at once he lifted his wings.
They swooshed stronger than before
and powerfully carried him up and away.

Modernity gave us an engineering mentality toward life. If life were a rushing river, we would not relish its roar or delight in its force and fierceness, but view it as a wasted resource. Thus we would build a dam to tame the wildness and a hydro-electrical plant to use its power. While we derived many visible benefits from this approach to life, we also paid an invisible price. When we treat nature, people, and even ourselves as a means of production, we become distanced and disconnected from life.

By contrast, a larger view suggests that life has its own intentions, just as the manager in *Fish* began to see the workers as having their own desires. When we approach life with interest rather than self-interest, then we become closer, more connected, and more engaged. When we are in our element we connect most deeply, not only with the uplifting aspects of life but also with the frightening ones. For the ugly duckling the water is his element; he comes alive when he dives and splashes, but he is also terrified when the water turns red with blood and when it later traps him in the ice. For us as human beings, our natural element may be poetry, physics, parenting, or policing, whatever work connects us to the universal.

As we dive into our element, the water of our life, we can learn five important lessons.

1. We are capable. When the mother duck first sees the odd-looking creature, she worries he may be a turkey chick. To test him she brings her brood down to the water, and fortunately the ugly one dives in right away and floats beautifully. "No, that's no turkey!" says the mother; "Look how nicely he's using his legs, and how tall he carries himself. He's my own all right!"

When we are in our element we are strong. For our work to be meaningful, we do not need to engage in righteous tasks or do *good* work, but we do need to do *our* work. We need to do something we care deeply about. When we are thus engaged we can become surprisingly capable and even extraordinary.

2. We are exposed. After flying over the fence, the duckling hid in the marsh, where he lay quietly. Two friendly wild geese approached him, but suddenly the hunt was on, the geese were killed, and "the water turned red as blood." Even worse, a fearsome hunting dog came crashing through the rushes and nearly frightened the duckling to death. Life in the wild is precarious.

When we care deeply about something, we open ourselves to pain. Those who love language may be pained by clichés that others find clever. Those who care about fairness are hurt by injustices others barely notice. When we dare to engage wholeheartedly, there is no immunity.

3. We are alive. Running across the field, the duckling finds safety with the cat and hen, who expect him to defer to their superior judgment. But the duckling now shows a surprising degree of backbone. He is not manipulated by guilt, intimidated by their bossiness, or persuaded by the hen's arguments. The duckling understands that the heart has its own reasons.

Most of us do not want to be seen as "difficult" or irrational, so we conform to the dominant culture. Yet, when we disregard our passion, we become listless. A couple of years ago I was in a funk. Then I heard the contemporary poet David Whyte say, "You only have to say exactly how you don't belong and you're already on your way home." Suddenly the floodgates opened up and I poured months of pent-up frustrations onto my computer.

When I subsequently reviewed my notes I could see how each comment implied a certain need, desire, or dream for the future. This reflection helped me later, when I chose to pursue my longing and had to deal with my own inner hen.

4. We get stuck. Back in the wild, the duckling faced a harsh winter. The frost was so severe the little creature had to use his legs all the time to keep the swimming hole open. "In the end he became so weak he lay quite still, and then he froze fast in the ice." By chance, a farmer saw him and saved him.

When we are in our element we may take on more than we can handle, be constantly on the go, and become overextended and trapped by our own success. Feeling we do not have enough time to become "difficult," we become frozen in our development. Then we need help to get unstuck. Reading something that warms our heart or having a long conversation with a friend may help us break the pattern.

5. We belong. In the fall, the duckling is both inspired and disturbed by the vision of the swans. In the spring, he is compelled to approach the swans, yet he is also terrified as they rush toward him. Finally, at the moment of truth, he sees his own reflection and recognizes his true essence. He knows where he belongs.

We belong when we do the work we love to do. We belong when we engage with people who share our passion or who encourage it. We belong when we experience what the playwright George Bernard Shaw describes as "the true joy in life": to be used for a purpose recognized by ourselves "as a mighty one." But often the idea of belonging scares the heck out of us, because when we give ourselves to something greater than our narrow self-interests we become vulnerable, we give up the illusion of being in control. This is not a trip where we can be assured safe passage.

While the idea of a quest may sound exciting, most of us would prefer to manage it like a business trip. We want a detailed agenda so we know how to prepare, we want a tight itinerary so we do not waste time, and we want no surprises. But if anyone were to give us such an itinerary we should beware. We would not be following *our* path but *theirs*.

We need to accept that life is risky. No one can guarantee us conventional success when we jump over the fence, run across fields, and spread our wings. But we can be sure that we will grow and that life will become richer, deeper, and more satisfying.

SOMETHING TO THINK ABOUT...

What voices do you need to leave behind? The judgmental voices of the duck yard or the sensible nagging of the hen?

What individuals or groups do you feel drawn to? Who would you love to learn from?

SOMETHING TO TALK TO YOUR COLLEAGUES ABOUT...

Have you had the experience of swimming with swans? What did you do? What was it like?

How can we help each other grow into our swan-like nature?

3

THE DUNG BEETLE

■

When we want status,
we look to promote ourselves.

■

THE DUNG BEETLE is a fast-paced and diverting adventure. Our bad-tempered beetle ventures into the world, faces many trials, and returns with all its prejudices intact. The creature manages this feat by doing what any self-respecting narcissist would do: When faced with information that challenges its inflated self-image, it simply reinterprets the facts. The dung beetle's dictum is, "Don't learn about yourself; just learn how to spin."

The trouble starts when the Emperor's horse gets gold shoes and the beetle gets brushed off. The status-conscious beetle is incensed. In its mind, it is as important as the horse and an injustice has been done. Refusing to face reality, the critter spends the whole tale and all its energy defending an illusion.

As you read the following summary or, if you prefer, the full tale, consider these questions: What draws you to some of the characters? What bothers you? Are you reminded of times when you preferred illusions to learning?

A SUMMARY OF THE TALE

The Emperor's mount was receiving gold shoes because it had carried the Emperor in battle, fought valiantly, and saved the Emperor's life.

When the blacksmith had finished attaching the gold shoes, the dung beetle crawled out, stuck out its thin legs, and said, "First the big ones, and then the little ones." "What do you want?" asked the blacksmith. "Gold shoes!" said the beetle. "But *why* is the horse getting gold shoes? Don't you understand it?" asked the smith. "Understand it?" yelled the beetle. In the beetle's opinion, the horse was a lazy creature that could not even feed and water itself, yet it was given preferential treatment. Infuriated, the beetle went off in a huff.

The dung beetle flew away from the stable and landed in a lovely flower garden where a ladybug exclaimed, "Isn't it lovely here?" The beetle dismissed her with, "Do you call this beautiful? There isn't even a pile of manure here!" Next it met a caterpillar that talked about its "deep sleep" and awakening as a butterfly. The beetle thought that was nonsense, so it ridiculed the larva and flew off feeling vastly annoyed.

After a night of pouring rain, the dung beetle overheard two frogs, who thought that those who didn't love such wet weather didn't love their country. When the beetle asked for directions, the frogs ignored him. Feeling offended, the beetle muttered, "I never ask a second time!" when it had already asked three times without getting an answer.

Eventually the beetle found a ditch and the company of its own kind. It boasted of coming from the Emperor's stables and being born with gold shoes, and soon afterward it was married. But, in just a few days it got bored and moved on.

After many more adventures, the beetle finally happened to fly back in through the stable's window, where it landed in the silky mane of the Emperor's horse. Trying to collect its wits, it muttered, "Here I am sitting on the Emperor's charger! What am I saying? Yes, now everything becomes clear!" Suddenly, the beetle was in great spirits. "The world is not so bad after all." *Why* was the Emperor's charger given gold shoes? Because the beetle was to be the rider!

DID YOU KNOW . . . *The Dung Beetle* is a

status-seeking and self-promoting creature. Although it comes from the lowliest background, it has delusions of grandeur. Much the same could be said about H. C. Andersen, except that his foolish fantasies came true.

H. C. Andersen's life is the quintessential Horatio Alger story. While such success stories were uncommon in the "new world," they were virtually unheard of in the old. Yet, in spite of a class-obsessed society and centuries-old prejudices, H. C. Andersen made his way in the world, drawing only on his innate talent and indomitable spirit. He enthusiastically pursued his art, and he was entertaining, socially astute, and unabashedly self-promoting.

The author had a great instinct for marketing. On his first trip abroad, he wrote a travel journal, which was published right after his return to Copenhagen. Here, H. C. Andersen introduced the readers to the great German cities, the rugged splendor of the Harz Mountains, and various German luminaries. In Dresden, H. C. Andersen attended the salon of Ludwig Tieck, next to Goethe the greatest literary figure in Germany at that time. He described how Tieck "asked if it was me who had written *The Journey by Foot*, and when I confirmed that was the case, he said something most amiable . . . ."[1] Thus, H. C. Andersen described a scenario that suggested he was already known in Germany and even read by their great artists. What H. C. Andersen failed to mention was that it had been he who had sent Tieck a copy of his book a year earlier, together with a lengthy, self-laudatory letter. It was a very effective ploy, and one that H. C. Andersen would repeat many times later in his life when visiting prominent artists.

H. C. Andersen made almost thirty trips abroad. His travel journals became very popular and are considered among his best works.

THE CLASSIC TALE

THE EMPEROR'S HORSE *got gold shoes, a gold shoe on each foot.*

Why did he get gold shoes? He was the most beautiful animal, had fine legs, intelligent eyes, and a mane that fell like a silken veil down over his neck. He had carried his master through clouds of gun smoke and a rain of bullets, and had heard the bullets sing and whistle. He had bitten and kicked, and had joined in the fighting when the enemy pressed closer. Then, with the Emperor, he had taken a great leap over the fallen enemy's horse, saved his Emperor's crown of red gold, and saved the Emperor's life, which was worth more than red gold. And for that reason the Emperor's charger got gold shoes—a gold shoe on each foot.

The dung beetle crawled out. "First the big ones, and then the little ones," it said, "though it's not the size that matters." And then it stretched out its thin legs.

"What do you want?" asked the blacksmith.

"Gold shoes!" replied the dung beetle.

"You're out of your mind!" said the blacksmith; "You want gold shoes too?"

"Gold shoes!" said the dung beetle. "Am I not as good as that

large beast, who needs to be waited on, groomed, looked after, fed, and watered? Don't I belong to the Emperor's stable too?"

"But why is the horse getting gold shoes?" asked the blacksmith, "Don't you understand?"

"Understand? I understand that it's disrespectful of me," said the dung beetle; "it's an insult, so now I'm going out into the wide world."

"Beat it!" said the blacksmith.

"Bully!" said the dung beetle. And then it went outside, flew a short distance, and landed in a most delightful little flower garden, where there was a scent of roses and lavender.

"Isn't it lovely here?" said one of the little ladybugs who flew about and had black dots on its red shield-like wings. "How sweet it smells, and how beautiful it is here!" "I'm used to better things!" said the dung beetle, "Do you call this beautiful? There isn't even a pile of manure here!"

So the beetle went on a bit farther, into the shade of a big cabbage; a caterpillar was crawling on it. "How wonderful the world is," said the caterpillar. "The sun is so warm. Everything's so delightful. And when one day I go to sleep and die, as they call it, then I shall awaken as a butterfly."

"Who do you think you are," said the dung beetle, "flying about like a butterfly! I come from the Emperor's stable, but no one there, not even the Emperor's charger who actually wears my cast-off gold shoes, has such notions. Get wings! Fly! Yes, let's fly!" And so the dung beetle flew. "I won't be annoyed, but it still annoys me."

Next it dropped down on a large spot of grass, where it lay for a little while and then fell asleep.

Suddenly there was a deluge, a downpour! With all that splashing, the dung beetle was awakened, and right away it wanted to dig itself down into the ground, but couldn't do it. It tumbled over, swam on its belly, and was turned over on its back.

There was no question of flying. It probably would not get out of this place alive, so it lay where it lay, and there it stayed.

When it let up a little, and the dung beetle had blinked the water out of its eyes, it caught a glimpse of something white. It was a piece of linen laid out to bleach. The beetle made its way there and crept into a fold in the wet linen. It was certainly not like lying in a warm pile of manure in the stable, but there was nothing better around. And so it stayed there a whole day and a whole night, and the rainy weather stayed too. At dawn the dung beetle came out. It was really fed up with the weather.

Two frogs were sitting on the linen, their eyes shining with sheer delight. "It's such wonderful weather!" said one. "It's so refreshing. And the linen collects the water so wonderfully. My hind legs tickle as if I were about to swim!"

"I would like to know," said the other, "if the swallow who flies so far and wide, if it, on one of its many trips abroad, has found a better climate than ours. Such gusts and such wetness! It's just as if one were lying in a wet ditch. If that doesn't make one happy, well then one certainly doesn't love one's homeland!"

"Have you never been in the Emperor's stables?" asked the dung beetle. "There it's both warm and fragrant. That's what I'm used to; that's my climate, but you can't take it with you on your travels. Isn't there a hotbed in the garden where people of high standing like myself can check in and feel at home?"

But the frogs did not understand the beetle, or did not want to understand it.

"I never ask a second time!" said the dung beetle, when it had already asked three times without getting an answer.

So it walked on a bit, and there lay a piece of a flowerpot. It shouldn't have been there, but lying the way it did it gave shelter. Several earwig families lived there. They did not need much space, only company. The females were especially endowed with moth-

erly love; so, each one's brood was the best looking and the brightest.

"Our son has become engaged," said one mother, "the sweet innocent! His greatest ambition is someday to climb into the ear of a minister. He is so adorably childish, and the engagement keeps him from running wild. That's such a comfort to a mother!"

"Our son," said another mother, "came out of the egg and was up to mischief right away. He's bursting with energy, he's sewing his wild oats. That's a great joy for a mother. Isn't that so, Mr. Dung Beetle?" They recognized the stranger by its shape.

"You're both right!" said the dung beetle, and so it was invited up into the living room, as far it could get under the piece of pottery.

"Now you must also see my little earwigs!" said the third and fourth of the mothers; "they are the dearest children and so much fun! They are never naughty, except when their stomachs hurt. But that happens so easily at their age!"

And so each mother talked about her brood, and the youngsters talked too, and they used the little tweezers they had on their tails to pull the dung beetle's whiskers.

"They're always up to something, those little rascals!" said the mothers, who reeked of motherly love. But all this bored the dung beetle, and so it asked if it was far from here to the closest hotbed.

"That's a long way out in the world, on the other side of the ditch," said the earwig. "I hope none of my children will ever go that far, for it would be the death of me!"

"Well, that's how far I'll try to get," said the dung beetle, and left without saying goodbye, for that is most polite, isn't it?

At the ditch it met several of its kin, all dung beetles.

"This is where we live," they said. "It's quite cozy. May we invite you to come down into the rich mud? Your journey must have worn you out."

"That it has," said the dung beetle. "I have been lying on linen in the rain, and cleanliness takes a lot out of me. I have also gotten rheumatism in the wing-joint by standing in the draft under a piece of pottery. It's most refreshing to be among my own kind."

"Do you come from the hotbed?" asked the oldest.

"Higher up than that," said the dung beetle. "I come from the Emperor's stable, where I was born with gold shoes. I'm traveling on a secret mission, but you must not question me about it, for I cannot say anything."

And then the dung beetle crawled down into the rich mud. There sat three young female dung beetles, and they giggled for they did not know what to say.

"They're not engaged," said the mother, and then they giggled again, but this time from embarrassment.

"I've not seen any more beautiful in the Emperor's stables," said the traveling dung beetle.

"Don't ruin my girls! And don't talk to them unless you have honorable intentions; but so you have, and I give you my blessing."

"Hurray!" said all the others, and then the dung beetle was engaged to one of them. First engagement, then marriage. After all, there was nothing to wait for.

The next day went quite well, the second went more slowly, but by the third day one had to think about food for the wife and possibly the little ones.

"I've let myself be taken by surprise," it said, "so I'll have to surprise them back!"

And so it did. Gone it was; gone the whole day, gone the whole night—and the wife was a widow. The other dung beetles said that this was a no-good vagabond they had taken into the family, and the wife was now a burden to them. "In that case she can sit as a maiden again, and as my child," said the mother. "Shame on that horrible wretch who abandoned her!"

In the meantime the beetle was on the move and had sailed across the ditch on a cabbage leaf. Later in the morning two people came by. They saw the dung beetle, picked it up, and twisted and turned it. They were both very learned, especially the young man. "Allah sees the black beetle in the black stone in the black mountain! Doesn't it say so in the Koran?" he asked. And then he translated the dung beetle's name into Latin and gave an account of its genealogy and habits. The older scholar voted against their taking it home with them, saying that they already had an equally good specimen there. That was not a very polite thing to say, thought the dung beetle, and so it flew out of his hand. It flew a good distance, its wings having dried out, and then it reached the greenhouse. Because one of the windows had been pushed open, it could easily slip in and dig down into the fresh compost.

"This is delicious!" it said.

Soon it fell asleep and dreamed that the Emperor's horse had taken a fall and that Mr. Dung Beetle had received the charger's gold shoes and the promise of two more. What a pleasure that was! Then the dung beetle woke up, crawled out, and looked up. How magnificent it was in the greenhouse! Large palms spread out up high, made transparent by the sun, and underneath grew lavish greenery and flowers that glowed red as fire, yellow as amber, and white as newly fallen snow.

"What an amazing abundance of plants! How good this will taste when it all begins to rot," said the dung beetle. "This is a great pantry. I expect some of my kin live here. I will go look for them and see if I can find some with whom I can associate. I have my pride, and that's my pride!" And then it walked around and thought about its dream about the dead horse and the gold shoes it had won.

All of a sudden, a hand grabbed the dung beetle. It was squeezed and twisted and turned.

The gardener's little son and his friend were in the hothouse, had seen the dung beetle, and were now going to have some fun with it. Placed in a grape leaf, it was put down into a warm trouser pocket, where it wriggled about. But the boy squeezed it with his hand and then walked quickly down to the big lake at the bottom of the garden. There the dung beetle was put in a broken wooden shoe with the top missing. A stick was fastened as the mast, and the dung beetle was tied to it with a woolen thread. Now it was the skipper and was going out sailing.

It was a very big lake, and the dung beetle thought it was a great ocean. It was so surprised that it fell onto its back with its legs kicking.

The wooden shoe sailed along with the currents in the water, but when the ship got too far away, then one of the boys would roll up his pant legs and go out and fetch it back. But then as it drifted off again, the boys were called, and called in earnest, so they hurried off and let the wooden shoe be a wooden shoe. It drifted ever farther from land, ever farther out. It was horrifying for the dung beetle, which could not fly because it was tied to the mast.

Then it was visited by a fly.

"What wonderful weather we're having," said the fly. "I can rest here and sun myself. A very comfortable place you have here."

"You're talking as if you had no sense. Can't you see that I'm tied up?"

"Well, I'm not tied up!" said the fly, and then it flew away.

"Now I know what the world is like," said the dung beetle. "It's a low-down world! I'm the only respectable creature in it! First they deny me gold shoes, then I have to lie on wet linen, have to stand in a draft, and finally they push a wife on me. Then, when I take a brisk step into the world to see how life could be, how it should be for me, along comes a human pup and puts me out on the raging sea. And all that while the Emperor's horse is walking about with gold shoes on! That's what bothers me the most. But you can't expect sympathy in this world. My life has been most interesting, only what good is that when no one knows about it? Then again, the world doesn't deserve to know. Otherwise it would have given me gold shoes in the Emperor's stable, when the charger was given shoes and I stuck out my legs. Had I been given gold shoes, I would have been a credit to the stable. Now it has lost me, and the world has lost me, everything is over!"

But everything was not over yet. A boat came along with young girls.

"A wooden shoe is sailing there," said one of them.

"There's a small creature tied to it," said the other.

They were right next to the wooden shoe, so they picked it up, and one of the girls took out a small pair of scissors and cut the woolen thread without harming the dung beetle. And when they came ashore, she put it down in the grass.

"Crawl, crawl! Fly, fly if you can!" she said. "Freedom is a wonderful thing."

And the dung beetle flew straight in through the open window of a large building and sank down exhausted into the long, silky mane of the Emperor's charger, who stood in the stable where he and the dung beetle belonged. The dung beetle clung to the mane and sat there for a short while and collected itself. "Here I am, sitting on the Emperor's charger! Sitting as the rider! What am I saying? Yes, now everything becomes clear! And it's a good idea and it's true. Why did the horse get gold shoes? The blacksmith also asked me about that. Now I see! It was for my sake the horse was given gold shoes!"

And then the dung beetle was in great spirits.

"How it clears the head to travel!" it said.

The sun shone on it, it shone so beautifully. "The world is not so bad after all," said the dung beetle. "You just have to know how to take it." Yes, the world was wonderful; the Emperor's charger had been given gold shoes because the dung beetle was to be his rider.

"Now I'll go down to the other beetles here and tell them how much has been done for me. I'll tell them of all the pleasures I have enjoyed on my trip abroad, and I'll say that now I'm staying at home until the horse has worn out his gold shoes!"

THE TALE AT WORK

The dung beetle is a self-absorbed, self-promoting, status-driven critter who prefers self-aggrandizing notions to dealing with facts. But we do not get gold shoes just by being full of ourselves, and we cannot build an authentic work life based on illusions. To become a valued player we need to be aware of our strengths and weaknesses, our drives and goals, and our emotional triggers. Not that our aim should be to suppress all beetle-like tendencies; after all, such energy and imagination can be very useful. The goal is to face ourselves and the current reality so we can develop the personal and professional mastery we need to succeed.

SWAGGERING BEETLES

Am I not as good as that large beast, who needs to
be waited on, groomed, looked after, fed, and watered?

One of the dung beetle's shortcomings is that it is rather full of itself, that it has no doubts about its own importance. In psychological terms, it is "excessively self-important," an egocentric critter, a narcissistic little bug.

The problem with narcissists is not so much that they overvalue themselves; it is that they devalue others. Thus no harm is done when the self-promoting beetle props itself up by boasting that it comes from the Emperor's stables. We do much the same when mentioning our connections to top schools and *Fortune* 500 firms, however tenuous. The trouble is that the beetle incessantly puts others down. It insists that the horse is useless because it can neither feed nor water itself; that the flowers in the garden smell of nothing compared to a nice whiff of dung; and that the damp ditch is uncomfortable compared to the moist heat of manure. The beetle does not compete by getting better than others, but by tearing others down. Like most narcissists, it does not use its clever talents to create, but to destroy.

At work, narcissists crave adulation more than relationships, they want their ideas applauded rather than examined, they want to be right rather than to learn, and they take the credit for successes while blaming others for failures. They will say either "The last project was a '10' because I rescued it" or "There was nothing wrong with my plan, they just didn't have the guts to implement it"—all depending on the outcome. They posture rather than perform.

Some self-absorbed individuals, unlike the beetle, *do* perform. While these people are equally full of themselves, they have no need to tear others down; instead they use their self-starting, self-promoting, and creative abilities constructively. Although these creatures are not narcissists in the purest sense of the word, anthropologist and psychoanalyst Michael Maccoby coined the term "productive narcissists" to describe them.

"Productive narcissists" are self-motivated, self-confident, innovative, and audacious in their goals. Their confidence is contagious, so people rally around them and carry out their plans. When productive narcissists make the right calls, the results can be rather brilliant. Unfortunately, if their positive press goes to their heads, they may begin to seek fawning and flattery instead of facts. Then they come to believe that they not only deserve the "gold shoes" but that they are entitled to them. They may think that the rules that apply to regular people do not apply to them, and even that the laws that govern lesser performers do not concern them. When productive narcissists come to see themselves as masters of the universe, they become isolated from reality and may take inordinate risks on behalf of the organization. As a result, even though their past successes may have been spectacular, their failures may be more so.

To evaluate whether you are overestimating or underestimating your abilities, try to draw up a list of your strengths and weaknesses. Then ask a few close friends or colleagues, people who know you well and whose opinions you trust, to create their lists. The comparison will give you a good reality check. Such self-awareness is central to good professional decisions.

An indication of good self-awareness is being able to talk comfortably about one's weaknesses and even have a sense of humor about one's limitations. One of my friends, for example, refers to his self-aggrandizing tendencies as his "Napoleon"; similarly, a former professor of mine would, after a weekend gambling in Las Vegas, talk about how he had let out "the king." We also see such humor in author Ashley Brilliant, who winks at our egocentric tendencies with book titles such as *Appreciate Me Now and Avoid the Rush* and *All I Want Is a Warm Bed, a Kind Word, and Unlimited Power*.

STATUS-DRIVEN BEETLES

"I never ask a second time!" said the dung beetle, when it had already asked three times without getting an answer.

Another concern about the beetle is its unrestrained need for status. The beetle is obsessed with the gold shoes; it covets the gold shoes. In the book *Driven*, Paul Lawrence and Nitin Nohria, professors at Harvard Business School, would describe this desire as being driven to acquire. Their research indicates that in addition to that drive, we are also intrinsically motivated to bond, learn, and defend. This can be a challenge for us human beings, for at times these drives are conflicting.

The beetle cares only about gold and status and is determined to defend its perceived importance. Its drives to bond and learn are stunted. It has no interest in long-term relationships, not even with its own kind, nor does it care about learning. Such one-dimensional individuals often become stubbornly attached to their view of the world and dismissive of others' viewpoints. For example, those who are extremely competitive often tell the "touchy-feely" types to "wake up and smell the coffee." They poke fun at diversity and synergy and insist such notions will not work "in the real world." On the other hand, one-dimensional "bonders" often view competition as primitive and cooperation as more evolved. They feel somewhat superior to ambitious colleagues, whom they see as cutthroat, selfish, and short-term in their thinking. Granted, they would say, the competitive players may bring in the results this quarter, but what about morals and morale? At least when nice people lose, they do so with integrity.

When we put down certain drives in others we also become distanced from those drives ourselves. By doing that we deny ourselves access to part of our human capabilities, part of our potential. Consequently we put ourselves at risk, for in today's ever-changing workplace it is no longer enough to have a competitive or cooperative advantage. Instead, we need to be very versatile, to draw on all four drives to gain the *adaptive advantage*. Just as we need to assess candidly our strengths and weaknesses, as mentioned in the discussion on narcissism, we also need to understand what drives us. What makes us happy? What turns us on? What motivates us to give our best effort? Only with such understanding can we create a meaningful work life.

BRISTLING BEETLES

"It's an insult, so now I'm going out into the wide world!"
"Beat it!" said the blacksmith; "Bully!" said the dung beetle.

As if the beetle did not have enough flaws, it is also unable to control its emotions. When the horse gets the coveted shoes, the dung beetle becomes green with envy, eaten by envy, and consumed with envy. The emotional turmoil is further compounded by the critter's narcissism, for it can see neither its own limitation nor the horse's merit. To the beetle this is an injustice, and feeling "justifiably" angry it now cuts a swath of negativity through the tale. While it may think its aggressive, antagonistic, and argumentative behaviors are a sign of strength, they only reveal its basic weakness.

Like the beetle, we tend to get upset when things do not go our way. When we feel unfairly treated or placed under undue pressure, we too may become short-tempered and belligerent, take offense at imagined insults, and go off in a huff. Or rather than vent our anger, we may "eat" it, become impatient and irritable, and then reach for the antacids to digest it.

If we want to become strong players in our ever-evolving economy, we need to understand our emotions. What triggers them? How do they play out? What is their effect on others? Do we want to manage them better? Again, having a sense of humor helps. For example, a former colleague made it safe to discuss his rare but fierce and angry outbursts by referring to his "evil twin."

While we often need to temper some emotions, we may want to encourage others. For example, many men were raised to suppress their tenderness, and many women were raised to curb their ambition, thus restricting their emotional range. When we manage to rekindle what once was rejected, we may become more emotionally balanced, more well-rounded, and more capable.

SELF-AWARE BEETLES

"I have my pride, and that's my pride!"

The dung beetles among us often have a stunning inability to see their own shortcomings, though others can list them in a minute. When succeeding, they have no need to change; when failing, others are to blame. Occasionally, however, reality rises up and hits them over the head with a two-by-four. This may be in the form of a serious illness, a traumatic event, or surprising feedback.

An elegant form of feedback taught the great cyclist Lance Armstrong a valuable lesson early in his career, which he describes in his book, *It's Not About the Bike*. As a young rider on the European circuit, he was an aggressive, loud-mouthed, in-your-face Texan and proud of it! He had no need to "bond" with the main group of riders. As a result, the other riders would cut him off, isolate him, make him ride slower, or weaken him by riding too hard and forcing him to keep up. Nothing, however, got to him.

Armstrong would also insult respected cyclists, like the day he surged right up to the Italian capo Moreno Argentin and challenged him. Taken by surprise, Argentin asked, "What are you doing here, Bishop?"—mistaking Armstrong for another American rider. Armstrong was incensed that the Italian did not even know his name. After a few expletives he said, "My name's Lance Armstrong, and by the end of this race you'll know it." Like the beetle, he was full of himself, bristling, and driven to win! Only, his mouth was bigger than his abilities. He lost that race.

A few days later Armstrong was riding a one-day race, which was better suited to his impatient and aggressive style. Being as thin-skinned as the beetle, Armstrong had not forgotten the "insult," and he went after Argentin again. In the final sprint among four riders, Armstrong was in the lead and Argentin lagged behind. Argentin saw he was unable to win, yet he did not want to lose to the loudmouthed American. A few feet before the finish line he braked and locked his wheels, thus making sure he came in fourth. Argentin did not want to stand next to Armstrong on the podium. Armstrong could not believe it. "What he was saying was that he didn't respect me. It was a curiously elegant form of insult, and an effective one."[2] The incident humbled Armstrong, and he learned to work *with* the group rather than against it, a much smarter use of his energy.

Later, cancer would teach Armstrong even harsher lessons about strength, humility, and patience. But while some of his rough edges were softened, he fortunately retained his fierce competitive nature. Drawing on a broader range of abilities, he moved from being merely a good rider to become a great one, winning the Tour de France a record number of times.

Rather than using feedback the way we should—to become more well-rounded and stronger performers—we often use it to soften people up and squeeze them into some preconceived corporate mold. This rubs me the wrong way. Were I to give the beetle some feedback, I would encourage its amazing imagination, single-minded focus, and self-promoting talents. Only, I would want it to stop squandering so much energy on illusions and to face a few essential facts. But what I would *not* want is to turn the beetle into a domesticated and empathic critter, reclining on a chaise lounge, eating candy. No! I would want it to do what Armstrong did: Manage the immature energy, integrate it, and become stronger! One can be self-aware and still swagger.

Not everybody needs to temper their beetle-like aggressive and angry energies, however. Some people need to learn to access them more. Such is the case with those of us who grew up in traditional communities where we were de-fanged, de-clawed, and raised to be nice.

SUPPRESSED BEETLES

*"If that doesn't make one happy, well then one
certainly doesn't love one's homeland!"*

We did not swagger in my hometown. Aggressive and ambitious people were perceived as being selfish, using sharp elbows, and stepping on others. Wanting status was a lamentable vanity, and being envious was immature. Instead of competition, we valued cooperation; instead of standing alone, we stood shoulder to shoulder; instead of looking out for number one, we looked out for one another; instead of signing contracts, we shook hands. We trusted one another for we played by the same rules. To the Danes, these rules are known as the Jante Law, which refers to the fictitious town Jante in a novel by Aksel Sandemose. The "Law" lists ten unspoken norms, including "You must not believe you are better than us," and "You must not believe that you know more than us."

Though Sandemose did not write about the Jante Law until 1933, these informal rules existed long before, and H. C. Andersen was well aware of them. To escape conformist pressures, H. C. Andersen traveled extensively, and he particularly basked in the attention he received in Germany. But the Copenhagen bourgeoisie did not want him to take too much pleasure in foreign places. Thus, some began to question his patriotism, a not-so-subtle warning that he'd better stay put. H. C. Andersen was wounded by the attacks, but responded in *The Dung Beetle* by putting the words of the self-righteous burghers into the mouths of the bigoted frogs. In the story the dung beetle hears the frogs praise a soggy and miserable morning, as they wonder whether the swallow, on one of its many travels to foreign countries, has ever found a better climate. The frogs insist that if one does not appreciate this wonderfully wet weather, then one *certainly* doesn't love one's own country. What an elegant way for H. C. Andersen to even the score!

Like most Danes, I learned to play down my ambitious and aggressive tendencies, though I rather enjoyed them in others. For example, I once worked with a number of super-competent colleagues with super-sized egos. One of them was particularly entertaining. His self-aggrandizing humor showed flickers of self-awareness, and his prickly e-mails made me laugh. While the *nice* side of me felt he behaved like a jerk, my suppressed beetle enjoyed his impertinence. Likely, I am captivated by New York City for the same reason. Being the self-proclaimed "capital of the world," this is one arrogant and ambitious city. New Yorkers even take pride in their do-you-have-a-problem-with-that attitude. But why live vicariously? Why not claim that energy in myself? Part of my fear was that it might overwhelm my "nice" personality. Could I play with aggressive and ambitious energies in ways that were safe for my self-esteem and appropriate for my self-image?

To experiment with ambition, I was fortunate to land in corporate America. Suddenly, what had been discouraged was encouraged, what had been a weakness was a virtue. Similarly, when it came to my experiments with anger, I was lucky to have married a Spaniard. Where I came from, everyone knew that getting the silent treatment was a sign of seething emotions, but when I used punitive silence with my Mediterranean husband, he totally missed it! He just thought it was nice that I was quiet. Unusual? Sure, but welcomed nonetheless. To communicate better I learned to express my frustration more forcefully, which was rather exhilarating for a while. In the end, however, it felt out of character, and I settled for an assertive but calmer way to express displeasure.

Let me be clear here. I am not advocating that readers who were raised to be nice now become nasty. I am saying that we can benefit from accessing the marginalized energy, integrate it, and become whole. We can be nice and still play to win.

THE FREE-AGENT REALITY

Freedom is a wonderful thing!

Spinning is a fact of life, and from job interviews to annual reports we give our version of the truth. But the sequence is important: First face the facts, and then do the creative positioning. The difference between a clever spin and beetle-like self-deception is the difference between using facts and denying them.

At the beginning of the story the blacksmith asks, "*Why is the horse getting gold shoes?*" The beetle refuses to deal with the facts, denies the horse's merit, and exaggerates its own. Next comes a series of adventures where the beetle could have learned a great deal about itself and the world. But rather than changing its self-image to fit with reality, it distorts reality (creates a fantasy) to fit its idea of itself.

Today, our workplace reality deals with downsizing, outsourcing, and offshoring, and we are foolish if we cling to fantasies of lifetime employment and linear career trajectories. We need to accept that, as free agents, our only security comes from developing a strong professional identity, our unique brand. In his book *Re-imagine!* Tom Peters stresses three essentials for creating such a robust professional brand: mastery, networking, and marketing.

Mastery is at the heart of our brand. The Emperor's charger did not receive gold shoes for simply doing his job; he threw himself into the battle and performed brilliantly. He was not just competent; he was extraordinary. Likewise, we need to master something others value and will pay for. To do that, we constantly need to learn, to hone our craft, and to keep building our professional portfolio.

On top of that, we need to tend relationships like never before. The dung beetle limits itself to the company of beetles, much as we often stick to our own corporate kin. It is true that we need strong relationships with our boss and coworkers, but they are not enough. We also need extensive professional and interdisciplinary relationships. Given the global economy, we even need international networks. The more others know who we are and what we can do, the more options we have and the more resilient we may be.

Finally, we need to position and promote ourselves. Brands are all about stories, and as the storyteller of our life we can create our own legend. But we do not become legendary by simply *saying* we are the greatest. We must *become* the greatest. When the world heavyweight champion boxer Muhammad Ali was on top of his game, he was also a charismatic figure. Both children and adults flocked to his side and, to top it all off, he was a genius at self-promotion. This was a winning formula, and the champ not only created a great brand: He became an icon. As Ali would say with a twinkle in his eye, "It ain't bragging if you can do it."

Of the three essentials, mastery is at the heart of our brand. But to master our craft we must first master ourselves. Self-mastery is built on awareness and choice. We need to become aware of our personal and professional talents and limitations, as well as our motives and emotions. As we strengthen our awareness, we can become more adaptive and resourceful. Only then are we truly free to choose, only then can we make good decisions.

To become "world champions" at our profession we need a personal manager who is alert to what makes us unique and what makes us tick: a manager who plays to our strengths, chooses great parts, and coaches us to give a masterful performance; a manager who helps us develop both self-mastery and professional mastery. This "personal manager" cannot be hired, though. Rather, it is the conscious part of ourselves, the part that is aware and makes the choices. With such a competent personal manager on our side, we have no need for illusions.

SOMETHING TO THINK ABOUT ...

How do you make it safe for others to challenge your ideas and decisions?

When was the last time you made a mistake? What did you learn? Did you end up adjusting your image of yourself?

SOMETHING TO TALK TO YOUR COLLEAGUES ABOUT ...

How do we discourage fawning and flattery and encourage a candid look at the facts?

What is the dominant drive in your department (to acquire, to bond, to learn, or to defend)? Is it different from other departments? If so, how does that affect interactions among departments?

4

THE NISSE AT
THE GROCER'S

■

When we are real,
we know who we are.

■

A "NISSE" IS ABOUT THREE FEET TALL, wears a red stocking cap, and wants to stay out of sight. Yet, though you never really see him, to Danish children he is very real. Most farms have their own nisse, and when the owner treats him well, the family does well. In return, all the nisse expects is a large bowl of porridge (warm rice pudding, sprinkled with sugar and cinnamon, and topped with a big lump of butter) on Christmas Eve. But the family must never try to get a glimpse of him, for then he will get hopping mad and retaliate.

The nisse in this story is loyal to his landlord, curious, and mischievous. As this practical little creature is awakened to the world of ideas, we get to examine our own needs for property and poetry, for food for belly and food for thought.

As you read the following summary or, if you prefer, the full tale, consider these questions: What do you appreciate about the active life in the shop? What do you like about the quiet and reflective space in the attic? Do you seek to have both?

A SUMMARY OF THE TALE

The student owned nothing. The grocer owned the whole house and could afford the Christmas porridge, so the nisse stuck with him.

One evening the student came to buy cheese. As he was leaving, the grocer's wife nodded "good evening," though she could do more than nod: She had the gift of gab! But the student was distracted by the wrapping paper, which was from an old poetry book. The grocer offered to sell the rest of the book to the student, who accepted and returned the cheese for the tattered book. The student said it would be a sin to tear up such a book and joked that the grocer knew no more of poetry than the tub where the old newspapers were kept. The nisse thought that was very rude!

At night the nisse borrowed the wife's gift of gab, and any object he put it on could then express itself as well as she did. He first put "the gab" on the tub and asked, "Is it really true . . . that you don't know what poetry is?" "Of course I know," said the tub. "It's the type of stuff that is written at the bottom of the page in the newspaper." The tub thought it contained more of it than the student. All the other things in the shop thought so too, and "what most agree on, must be respected."

The nisse then went up the stairs to teach the student a lesson. But when he peeked through the keyhole, the student was reading from the tattered book and the room was filled with wonderful images and beautiful melodies. "This is amazing!" said the nisse. "I think I'll stay with the student!" But then he remembered that the student could not afford the porridge, so he went back down to the grocer.

But the nisse was no longer satisfied with the wisdom and intelligence in the shop, and every night he went to peek at the keyhole, where he was overcome by a sense of grandeur. But when the light went out in the student's room, he got cold and hurried back to the shop. And when it was Christmas and the nisse received his porridge, the grocer was definitely the best.

One night the street was threatened by a fire and all ran to rescue their most precious possessions. The wife reached for her earrings, the grocer ran for his bonds, and the nisse dashed up to the attic, where the student stood by the window and watched the blaze across the street. The nisse grabbed the book and rushed out onto the roof. It was clear where his heart lay. But when the fire had been put out, the nisse calmed down and thought, "I can't quite give up the grocer because of the porridge!" And so he decided to partake of both.

DID YOU KNOW . . .

The "nisse" shares some traits with other elf-like creatures like the pixie, gnome, or hobgoblin, but he is unique to Nordic folklore. The nisse was believed to take up residence on a farm, and if he was content he would bless the farm with many children, good health, good crops, and prosperity (much like the gods of the hearth in other pagan religions). Thus it was said of a wealthy farmer that he had a happy nisse. In return, the nisse expected to be treated with respect and given regular food offerings.

The nisse was depicted much like a farmer used to look in the Middle Ages, with gray beard, gray clothes, and a red stocking cap. He was old, short, and was said to smoke a pipe and like a good game of cards. The nisse was particularly helpful with the animals, but he might also take shortcuts to prosperity and steal from neighboring farms. Being rather irritable, the nisse would get upset over the slightest offense. When that happened the animals would get sick, the milk would run sour, and the crops would wither. When crossed, the nisse always evened the score.

The first record of a nisse dates back to 981 in Iceland, when a nisse was gotten rid of with prayers and holy water. But in the 16th and 17th centuries the clergy were still dealing with the "farm dweller." It appears that, though people were Christians and said their prayers, they also wanted to take care of their nisse . . . just to keep their bases covered.

In the 19th century the nisse underwent a radical makeover. This began when the Danish artistic community in Rome, a group H. C. Andersen knew well from his travels to Italy, used nisse-like paper cuttings to decorate for Christmas. In just a few years, this new image of the nisse gained popularity. Thus he became shorter, fatter, safer, and nicer, and he even acquired a wife. He was brought out of the barn and into middle-class living rooms, becoming a Santa Claus–like symbol for Christmas.

THE CLASSIC TALE

THERE WAS A REAL STUDENT *who lived in the attic and owned nothing. And there was a real grocer who lived on the ground floor and owned the whole house. The nisse chose to be with the grocer, and every Christmas Eve he got a big bowl of porridge with a large lump of butter! The grocer could afford it. So the nisse stayed in the store, which was most instructive.*

One evening the student came in through the back door to buy candles and cheese. He had no one to send, and so he came himself. He got what he asked for, paid for it, and the grocer and his wife nodded "good evening," although the wife was a woman who could do more than nod: She had the gift of gab! The student nodded back and then stood there, caught up in the reading of a leaf of paper that had been wrapped around the cheese. It was a page torn from an old book that should never have been ripped apart, an old book full of poetry.

"There's more of that book left," said the grocer, "I gave an old woman some coffee beans for it, and if you give me eight shillings you can have the rest of it!"

"Thank you," said the student. "Let me have the book instead of the cheese! I can eat my bread and butter without anything else on it. It would be a sin to have the whole book torn to bits and

pieces. You're an extraordinary man, a practical man, but you don't understand poetry any better than that tub!"

It was a rude thing to say, especially about the tub. But the grocer laughed, and the student laughed, for it was said as a sort of joke. But the nisse was annoyed that anyone would dare say such a thing to the grocer, who was the landlord and sold the best butter.

At night, when the store was closed and everyone was in bed except the student, the nisse went and borrowed the wife's gift of gab; she did not use it while sleeping. When he put it on any object in the room, that object would get voice and speech and be able to express its thoughts and feelings just as well as the wife expressed hers. But only one at a time could have it, which was a good thing, for otherwise they would all have talked at once.

First the nisse put the gift of gab on the tub, which was filled with old newspapers. "Is it really true," he asked, "that you don't know what poetry is?"

"Sure I know," said the tub. "It's the sort of thing at the bottom of the newspaper that is often cut out! I should think I have more of it in me than the student, and I'm only a humble tub compared to the grocer!"

Then the nisse put the gift of gab on the coffee grinder, and that sure got it going! He then put it on the butter measure and then on the money drawer. They all had the same opinion as the tub, and what most agree on, must be respected.

"Now the student's going to get it!" thought the nisse as he went very quietly up the kitchen stairs to the attic where the student lived. The light was on. The nisse peeked through the keyhole and saw the student reading from the torn book he got from downstairs. How bright it was in there! From the book came a clear beam of light, which turned into a trunk, a mighty tree that grew very tall and spread its branches far out over the student. Each leaf was fresh, and each flower was the head of the loveliest girl, some with eyes that were dark and sparkling and others with eyes that were amazingly blue and limpid. Each fruit was a shining star, and the loveliest song filled the air.

No, the little nisse had never imagined such beauty, let alone seen or felt it. So he remained standing on his toes and looked and looked until the light went out. The student had likely blown out the lamp and gone to bed. But the little nisse kept standing there as the song continued softly and gently, like a lovely lullaby for the student who had lain down to rest.

"This is amazing!" said the little nisse. "I never expected this! I think I'll stay with the student!" But after thinking about it—and sensibly so—he said with a sigh: "But the student has no porridge!" and he left; yes, he went back down to the grocer. It was a good thing he did! The tub had almost used up the wife's gift of gab by speaking everything that was written on one side of the papers inside it. It was just about to turn and go over everything that was on the other side, when the nisse came and took the gift of gab back to the wife. Yet from then on the whole store, from the money drawer to the kindling, took their opinions from the tub. They held it in such esteem and had such faith in it that later, when the grocer read "The Art and Theater Reviews" out loud from his evening Times, they all thought it came from the tub.

But the little nisse could no longer sit quietly and listen to all the wisdom and intelligence down in the shop. As soon as the light shone down from the attic, its rays drew him up there like strong anchor ropes, and he had to go and look through the keyhole. He was then overwhelmed by a sense of awe, much like the way we feel about the great ocean waves when God strides across them in a storm. He burst into tears, not quite knowing why he cried, for they were tears of happiness! How wonderful it would be to sit with the student under that tree! But that could not be, so he was content at the keyhole. He was still standing there in the cold corridor, when the autumn wind blew down from the trap door to the roof. It was cold, very cold, but the little nisse did not notice it until the light was put out in the attic and the melody died away in the wind. Brrrr! He was freezing, so he snuck back down to his cozy corner, which was so comfortable and convenient. And when the Christmas porridge came with a big lump of butter, yes, then the grocer was the most important to him.

Once, in the middle of the night, the nisse woke up because of a terrible noise on the shutters. People outside were pounding on them! The night watchman whistled! There was a big fire, and the whole street was in flames! Was it here in their house or at the neighbor's? Where? How terrifying! The grocer's wife was so befuddled that she took off her gold earrings and put them in her pocket, just so she could save something. The grocer ran to get his bonds, and the servant girl ran to get her silk mantilla, which she had been able to buy for herself. All wanted to save the best they had, and the little nisse wanted to do the same.

In a couple of leaps he was up the stairs and inside the room of the student, who was standing quite calmly by the open window, looking out at the fire in the courtyard across the street. The little nisse grabbed the wonderful book from the table, put it inside his red cap, and clasped it with both hands; the greatest treasure of the house was saved! And then he rushed out onto the roof all the way up to the top of the chimney. There he sat, illuminated by the burning house across the street, and with both hands he still held on tight to his red cap, where the treasure was. Now he knew for sure where his heart lay, to whom he really belonged. But then, once the fire was put out and he had collected himself, he said, "I'll share myself between them! I can't quite give up the grocer because of the porridge!"

And that was quite human! The rest of us also go to the grocer—for the porridge!

THE TALE AT WORK

The nisse enjoys the activity in the grocer's shop, a place of commerce, news, and noise. Just like life in the shop, our days tend to be filled with talk and excitement. We often start the morning with the news, catching up on the latest wars, corruption, business, and sports. On top of that, everything is doused with advertising images of what we ought to watch, wear, think, feel, and do.

In addition, people around us place incessant, and often conflicting, demands on our time. We should buy a house in the suburbs; attend all the kids' games; be hard workers, team players, and top performers; and be candid, kind, and constructive to boot.

With so many voices clamoring for our attention, we cannot hear our own. Only when we tune out the noise can we tune into ourselves. Only when we are free from the opinions of others can we articulate our own.

As we follow the nisse in this story, we will consider our everyday, pay-the-rent kind of life, as well as the ideal one. Do we see them as conflicting or complementary? Might they inform and enrich each other?

THE ACTIVE LIFE

There was a real grocer who lived on the ground floor
and owned the whole house. The nisse chose to be with the grocer.

The practical voice in our head is a no-nonsense voice: Get a *good* education, hold down a *good* job, make a *good* living, and enjoy the *good* life. That's it! Life is not that complicated. That is, as long as you curtail your nisse-like curiosity.

Like the grocer, many of us thrive on the busyness of "the shop." Personally, I love the bustling of a growing company and the pulse of New York City, the quintessential marketplace. Today the shop is global and open 24/7. The news and the next deal are just a click away.

To be players in the global workplace, we go to a good school and study the pages that will be on the exam. We pick a reputable firm, learn the right competencies, and hit targets. We wrap ourselves in the right brands, cars, neighborhoods, and schools for the kids. Life is linear and we are in control! Or, could it be that we are just conforming? Could it be that we live by the dictum of the shop, that "what most agree on, must be respected"?

When I look back, I have been surprised by just how many of my choices have been conventional ones. I should have noticed, as my life came to look more like the lives of my parents and peers. Was I really making "free" choices, or was I defaulting to preprogrammed settings? Let me give you an example. Years ago, I had a great job, I was "up and coming," and my success was reflected in possessions and property. Suddenly my husband's industry faced a downturn, and his company paid people off to leave. Because he had already thought of going back to school, this seemed like a great time for a change, and when he was admitted to Harvard Law School we thought it was worth the move. Therefore, we sold our houses, cars, washers, driers, and refrigerators in California, and moved cross-country and into an "attic" in Cambridge, Massachusetts.

Unexpectedly, I loved our new life. There was no brush to clear, no house or pool to clean, and no cars to maintain. When something in our small apartment needed fixing, we just called the super. I felt liberated! I was amazed to discover how our possessions had come to possess so much of our time, and I was surprised to realize that the dream of home ownership was not even my dream.

Based on what we learned then, we have continued to live much like students. When we think of making a major financial commitment we ask, for example, "Would we rather live close to Central Park (which I would love to do) or have financial freedom?" Freedom wins every time. As a result, my husband and I can afford the time for creative projects, for him his passion for music and for me this book. Granted, our *standard* of living does not impress anyone, but our *quality* of life is terrific.

For many of us, the problem is not that we want the good life; the problem is that we come to believe that our version of the good life is the right life. This happens when we read only the publications that cater to our interests and watch only the programs that confirm our existing opinions. Then, in the end, poetry is reduced to wrapping paper, information is confused with "wisdom," and we all say the things that "most agree on."

I do believe that many workplace blunders and unprincipled behaviors could be prevented if more "grocers," in addition to heeding the advice of touted business leaders, would also engage with the "students" among us. We need to spend some time genuinely exploring the moral and ethical dilemmas of everyday life, so that we can consider not only what might be the most efficient thing to do, but also what would be the right thing to do.

THE THOUGHTFUL LIFE

There was a real student who lived in the attic and owned nothing.

The practical nisse likes to be associated with the grocer, for he is a man of property. The student's life seems shabby. Yet the penniless student appears to have everything he needs. When the student exchanges the cheese for a tattered book, thus accepting to eat his bread and butter without anything else on it, he seems satisfied with the deal. Unconcerned with money, he has time to think, to delve into the great thoughts, to explore universal ideals, to contemplate the meaning of life.

When the nisse goes up to the attic, intending to teach the student a lesson, it is the nisse who is in for a surprise. Encountering the student's world, the nisse is overwhelmed by such a sense of grandeur that he can barely find the words to describe it. What could have had such an impact on this practical little creature? Was the nisse touched by the power of truth, courage, compassion, or beauty? Was he moved by thoughts of the eternal? Was he affected by the rousing ideals of liberty, equality, and justice for all, those "impractical" notions that transformed old nations and gave birth to new ones?

Even though the nisse is swept away by his discovery, as soon as the light is out and the vision disappears, he is hit by reality. While the ideal way of life may be inspiring, usually it does not keep a roof over our heads. Yet, life is about more than ever-greater efficiencies and endless to-do lists. Isn't it?

Like the grocer, "students" also have their weaknesses, and they are particularly at risk of becoming sanctimonious. This sneaks out when the student says, "It would be a sin to have the whole book torn to bits and pieces." The word *sin* suggests a self-righteousness typical of the centuries-old condescending attitude that many educated people had toward the masses, an attitude that suggested it was nobler to feed the mind than to feed the community.

In addition to developing a somewhat supercilious attitude, students also risk becoming too conceptual, too theoretical, and too removed from "the real world." Just as the grocer could learn much in the attic, so the student could benefit from spending some time on the ground.

Many of us leadership, human-resource, organizational-change professionals have a deep belief in human beings and their potential. But Abraham Maslow noted in his book, *Maslow on Management*, that we often become smug and pious about our theories. Maslow recommended that we instead spend time in the shop, where our theories can be tested by the reality of tough targets, tight budgets, and firm deadlines.

Similarly, timeless philosophical ideas are far more meaningful when we can use them to tackle real workplace issues such as diversity, offshoring, or executive pay, issues where a deeper understanding can help us make better decisions. This is the idea behind the Aspen Institute's seminars, where leaders from all walks of life use the work of great thinkers to tackle chronic societal and business challenges.

THOUGHTFUL ACTION

"I'll share myself between them! I can't quite give up the grocer because of the porridge!" And that was quite human!

The grocer enjoys life in the shop, the coming and going, the bargaining, the measuring, the money. This is the active life! Our priorities favor property, so when the fire threatens we save the earrings and bonds.

By contrast, the student likes the solitary life in the attic and the company of great minds. This is the thoughtful life. Yet, this life may become too distanced from the "real world." When fire threatens the street, for example, the student stands calmly by the window and watches—he is just an observer.

The little nisse belongs to both worlds. At first he is comfortable in the shop, but when his mind is stretched by great ideas, he is no longer content in there. He wants his comforts, but he is also drawn by the light in the attic. During the fire the nisse forgets all about the porridge. Instead, he runs up to the attic, tucks the tattered book into his red stocking cap, and rushes out onto the roof and all the way up to the chimney. There he sits and holds on to his cap with both hands. He knows his heart! But then, when the fire has been put out and the nisse has calmed down, he remembers just how much he likes porridge. Here, above both the shop and the attic, everything becomes clear. He does not need to choose sides; he will partake of both.

The wording of the original Danish language makes the ending somewhat ambiguous. H. C. Andersen uses the Danish word *dele*, which can be translated in two ways, one to suggest that the nisse would "divide" himself between the two worlds and the other that he would "share" himself between them. This is an important nuance. The first translation, the most commonly found, sees the realities as conflicting; the second, which I prefer, allows for possible integration.

The educator Parker Palmer writes about the contrast of contemplation and action in *The Active Life* and suggests that people deal with apparent opposites in different ways. We often start by keeping them separated, while later we may alternate between them, to hopefully end up looking for ways to integrate the two. A proponent of integration, Palmer hyphenates "contemplation-and-action," suggesting that one cannot exist without the other.

When seeing contemplation and action as opposites, we choose sides in the tug of war between them. We exacerbate the problem when we demonstrate our allegiance to one side by belittling those from the other side as either "irrelevant, ivory-tower elitists" or "greedy, self-serving hustlers." At the beginning of the tale, the grocer and the student live in separate worlds, and the nisse has chosen sides. The grocer is the winner, for he is the landlord and sells the best butter; the student has nothing and ought to know his place. When the student tells a joke at the grocer's expense, the nisse becomes vastly annoyed and is ready to teach the student a lesson. Interestingly, it is the nisse who learns the most as he begins to see the value of both worlds.

Instead of choosing one of the apparently conflicting opposites and looking down on the other one, we can begin to appreciate both. We may for example divide ourselves between them, by giving most of the week to practical matters and keeping Sundays for contemplation, or by pushing for months on a stressful assignment and then going fishing or backpacking. This is what the nisse does when he spends the day in the cozy shop and the evening in the attic. Both places are important, but neither touches the other.

But what if property and poetry were complementary, two halves of a greater whole? Then each side would complement and enrich the other. Then the tension might hold creative solutions rather than tearing us apart. The words "I will share myself between them" suggest that the nisse accepts the tension. He does not get disillusioned with himself for wanting the porridge, nor does he have a need to rush to a premature solution. He accepts that the two are part of his experience and that he needs to find his own way to hold both of them. He is refreshingly real.

A few months ago, my then six-year-old niece was equally transparent in examining her motives. During dinner, she asked why I was a vegetarian. My sister-in-law responded that it was because "Mette feels bad about killing animals." Ida pondered this while she kept chewing on a piece of chicken. Then she looked at me and said with great earnestness, "I also feel bad about killing animals . . . but I *really* like chicken." I was delighted by her response. She accepted the inconsistency and was disarmingly honest. By living with the tension instead of forcing the issue, she can grow into an answer that will be uniquely hers. She has plenty of time.

Like the nisse, we may have an experience where we become awakened to a life beyond the material. This may be caused by a serious illness or a senseless tragedy, or by a life-transforming workshop where we rappel down cliffs or walk across burning coals. For a short while everything is illuminated, everything is clear. We know our heart, and we feel resolved. Often, however, when the impact of the event softens and the glow wears off, we tend to revert to old behaviors and berate ourselves for our lack of commitment.

But why force an immediate choice between some romanticized ideal and our familiar ways of acting? Why must we solve the conflict right away? It is far better to stay with the tension a little longer. Granted, it is uncomfortable, but it is also a wonderfully creative space. By living for a while with the apparent conflict, we can look for ways in which each side may inform the other, and then we can grow into our very own *real-and-ideal* answer.

Some of the most influential people feel at home both in the grocer's shop and in the attic. Peter Drucker is behind some of the most practical management improvements of the twentieth century, and he is always learning something new. Since his early thirties, Drucker has been picking different subjects (such as international relations and law, the history of social institutions, or Japanese art) and then studying each topic intensely for three to four years. These studies have informed his practice and made him one of the most insightful management thinkers of our times. Drucker exemplifies the idea that nothing is as practical as a good theory. He is a model of thoughtful action.

Each of us needs to recognize where we are in our development. Do you see the ideal life as separate from your active, to-do-list kind of life? Do you exhaust yourself in the real world and use the other to recover? What timeless ideals rouse your emotions? Do you let enduring ideas inform your everyday choices? The more you draw on both the practical and the ideal, the more you will create your own solutions. The more you integrate the two, the wiser you will be.

SOMETHING TO THINK ABOUT . . .

When have you used moral principles to make practical decisions?

Whom do you consider to be successful and thoughtful?

SOMETHING TO TALK TO YOUR COLLEAGUES ABOUT . . .

What is it that most agree upon in your organization and that you automatically should respect?

What is the purpose of learning? To learn to think for yourself? To learn something practical? Maybe both?

5

THE FIR TREE

■

When we are restless,
we long for something else.

■

THE FIR TREE is a parable about life. It is a tragic tale—
not because the tree dies, but because it never really lived. Preoccupied with thoughts about the future or the past, it is never fully
present.

The story touches on something that is fundamental to a
happy life: the ability to be aware of and appreciate the moment.
It encourages us to be less concerned with what might be and
enjoy what is; to put our plans aside more often and savor the
moment; to heed our grandparents' advice and count our blessings.

Enjoying the moment is rather simple. It does not require extra
time, effort, or courage. All it takes is awareness and appreciation.
Yet, most of us do not do it. The questions are, What stops us
from being present right now? and, How can we live more fully?

As you read the following summary or, if you prefer, the full
tale, consider these questions: Are you likely to be preoccupied
rather than present? Do you postpone your life, thinking that
once you lose weight, get a new car, or get over the next deadline
. . . then life will be worth living? Do you tend to reminisce about
the good old days?

A SUMMARY OF THE TALE

Out in the woods there was a pretty little fir tree. The tree only wanted to grow up and get away, so it did not appreciate the sun and the fresh air. When it heard about masts on sailing vessels, it thought, "How I wish I were big enough to sail across the ocean!" Later it learned about the splendor of Christmas trees, and then the restless little tree couldn't wait for Christmas.

At last the fir tree was felled. The ax cut deep into its marrow, and the tree felt very sad about leaving home. But it became excited again when it was brought inside a beautiful room. Servants decorated it with candles and sweets saying, "Tonight it's going to shine!" and the fir tree thought, "Oh, if only tonight were here! What will happen then?"

Finally the candles were lit. The tree was splendid, but it was afraid to move even the slightest bit. Then people joined hands and danced around the tree, which kept thinking, "What're they doing? What's going to happen?" Finally the candles burned down and a little man told a story about Klumpe-Dumpe, who fell down the stairs and still got the Princess. The tree loved the story and then thought about how it would shine again the next day and how it would then enjoy its magnificence to the fullest.

But the next morning the fir tree was put up in the loft and left alone with its thoughts. Much later some curious mice came by, and the fir tree told them about its youth in the forest. The mice exclaimed, "My, how much you've seen! How happy you must have been!," and the tree realized that its time in the forest had been very pleasant. Then it told them about Christmas Eve, and the story it had heard about Klumpe-Dumpe. "Ooh!" said the little mice, "How happy you've been!" The tree thought that the good times would come again, and, like Klumpe-Dumpe, it too might get a Princess.

One night two rats showed up. They wanted to hear about pork and lard, and they were bored by the tree's tales. Then the mice didn't think so much of the stories either and stayed away. Now the tree missed the little mice and thought, "It was really quite lovely when those lively little mice sat around me and listened to what I had to say." It resolved to enjoy itself fully when it was taken out again.

Finally, the tree was brought out into the yard and felt the fresh air and the sun. "Now I shall live!" the tree cried out joyfully and spread its branches . . . only to see how withered and dry they had become. It was ashamed of its ugliness and thought, "If only I had enjoyed myself while I could!"

In the end, the fir tree was chopped into pieces and burned under the big kettle. And with every spark it sighed, "It's all over! All over!"

DID YOU KNOW ... December 1844 saw

the publication of *The Fir Tree*. Increasingly confident about the fairy tale genre, H. C. Andersen wrote to his friend H. C. Ørsted, the scientist who discovered electromagnetism, "I wonder what people will say about them in twenty years time! I don't think they will have been forgotten."[1]

Like the author, the fir tree was never content, always dreaming of greater glory or nostalgically reliving the past. The biographer Jackie Wullschlager, who focused on the author's more neurotic traits and desperate need for approval, calls this story "as precise a fantasy self-portrait as he ever composed, tragic and self-pitying in its witty self-recognition."[2]

The young Hans Christian had a lovely voice and quite a flair for the dramatic. He loved to sing and recite at small parties in the provincial Odense, and in the process he earned a few coins. Eventually the fourteen-year old boy had enough for the fare to Copenhagen.

The urchin had been in the capital only twelve days when he talked his way into the home of the Royal Theater's choir director, where several of Copenhagen's luminaries had gathered for dinner. The boy's untutored and rather ridiculous performance surprised this cosmopolitan group, yet his talent and passion touched them. They decided to sponsor this curiosity and passed the plate around to create a modest stipend. Years later, the renowned author would still perform for his supper when he, as a guest at manor houses, would give readings after dinner.

Underlying the story of the tree's desire to shine, Wullschlager observes an almost existential and "deeply ingrained pessimism, suggesting not only the mercilessness of fate but the pointlessness of life itself, that only the moment is worthwhile."[3] Maybe this was in the air at that time, for Søren Kierkegaard, the founder of existential philosophy, was a contemporary of H. C. Andersen.

THE CLASSIC TALE

OUT IN THE WOODS *there was a pretty fir tree. It had a good spot, it could get sun, had plenty of air, and all around grew many taller friends, both fir and pine. But the little tree was very impatient to grow. It did not think about the warm sun or the fresh air, and it did not care for the farmers' children who walked about prattling when they were out picking strawberries and raspberries. Often they would come with a bowl completely full or have strawberries strung on a straw, and then they sat next to the little tree and said, "Oh, what a pretty little tree!" But the tree did not want to hear that at all.*

The next year the tree's trunk had grown a stretch taller, and the year after it was taller still. With a fir tree you can always see how many years it has been growing by counting its joints.

"Oh, if only I were a great big tree like the others," sighed the little tree. "Then I'd spread my branches way out and from my top I would see far out into the wide world! The birds would then nest in my branches, and when the wind blew, I could nod with such dignity, just like the others over there."

The tree took no pleasure at all in the sunshine, the birds, or the red clouds, which morning and evening drifted overhead.

When it was winter and the sparkling white snow was lying all around, a little hare would often come and leap right over the little tree—oh, that was so annoying! But two winters passed, and by the third winter it was so big that the hare had to hop around it. Oh, to grow, to grow, to become tall and old, that was the only enjoyable thing in this world, thought the tree.

In the fall the woodcutters would come and cut down some of the largest trees. They came every year. The young fir tree, which by now was quite grown, trembled when that happened, for the great, majestic trees crashed down with a groan. Their branches were chopped off, which made them look quite naked, so long and slender you could hardly recognize them. Then they were put onto wagons, and horses hauled them away out of the forest.

Where were they going? What happened to them?

In the spring, when the swallow and the stork came, the young fir asked them. "Do you know where those trees are taken? Have you met them?"

The swallows knew nothing, but the stork looked thoughtful, nodded his head, and said, "Well, I think so. I came across many new ships when I flew back from Egypt, and the ships had magnificent tree masts. I dare say it was them, for they smelled of fir; they told me to say hello. They hold their heads up high, very high!"

"Oh, if I just were big enough to fly across the ocean! What is it actually, this ocean? What does it look like?"

"Well, that's very hard to explain," said the stork, and then it walked away.

"Rejoice in your youth," said the sun's rays, "rejoice at your fresh growth, the youthful life that's in you."

And the wind kissed it, and the dew wept tears over it, but the young fir tree did not understand.

When it was close to Christmas, some very young trees were chopped down, even ones that were not as big or as old as the fir tree. The tree was restless, and all it wanted was to get away. Those young trees they took were the very most beautiful ones, and they still had all their branches when they were put on the wagons and the horses carted them away out of the wood.

"Where do they go?" asked the fir tree. "They're no bigger than I am, and there was even one that was much smaller. Why do they get to keep their branches? Where do they go?"

"We know! We know!" chirped the sparrows. "Down in the city, we've looked through the windows, and we know where they go! Oh, they receive the greatest glory and splendor one can imagine! Through the windows we saw that they plant them in the middle of the warm room and they decorate them with the loveliest things: gilded apples, honey cakes, toys, and many hundreds of candles!"

"And then?" asked the fir tree, trembling in all its branches. "And then? What happens then?"

"Well, we haven't seen more than that, but it was magnificent!"

"I wonder if I'm meant for such a splendid journey," the tree cried with joy. "That's even better than going across the ocean. How I suffer from longing! If only it were Christmas! Now I am as tall and wide as the others that were taken away last year. Oh, if only I were on the wagon already, if only I were in the warm living room with all that glory and splendor! But, what then? Well, then something even better must happen, something even more beautiful. Why else would they decorate me like that? Something even greater, even more magnificent must happen. But what? Oh, how I suffer, how I long for something! I don't know what's the matter with me."

"Enjoy me," said the air and the sunlight, "enjoy your fresh youth out in the open."

But the tree did not enjoy it at all. It grew and grew, and through winter and summer it stood green, dark green. People who saw it said, "That's a beautiful tree," and at Christmas time it was the first one to be felled. The ax cut deep into its marrow.

The tree fell to the ground with a sigh. It felt pain, it felt faint, and it had no thoughts of happiness at all. The tree was very sad to be leaving home, the very spot where it had grown up, because it knew that it never again would see its dear old friends, the small bushes and flowers that grew all around, and maybe not even the birds. The going away was not pleasant at all.

The tree did not notice anything more until it was in the courtyard, unloaded with the other trees, and heard a man say, "That one is magnificent! We don't want any tree but that one!"

Then came two servants in fine livery and carried the fir tree into a lovely, large room. All around on the walls hung portraits, and by the large, tiled stove stood two great big Chinese vases with lions on the lid. There were rocking chairs, silk sofas, large tables stacked with picture books, and toys worth hundreds times hundreds of dollars—at least the children said so. The tree was propped up in a small barrel filled with sand, but no one could see it was a barrel, for they had draped green cloth around it, and it stood on a large colorful rug.

Oh, how it trembled! What was going to happen? Then both the servants and the young ladies walked around it and decorated it. On a branch they hung small nets cut from colorful paper, each net filled with sweets; gilded apples and walnuts hung as if they had grown on the tree; and over a hundred red, blue, and white little candles were attached to the branches. Dolls that looked as lifelike as human beings—the tree had never seen anything like them before—were hung among the greenery; and at the very top they placed a large star of gold tinsel. It was splendid, absolutely and uniquely splendid.

"Tonight," they all said, "tonight it's going to shine!"

"Oh!" thought the tree, "if only tonight were here! If only the candles were soon lit! Then what happens? I wonder if the trees from the forest will come and look at me. I wonder if the sparrows will fly up to the window. I wonder if I will grow roots here and stay decorated both winter and summer."

Well, little did the tree know. But it had a barkache from sheer longing, and a barkache is just as bad for a tree as a headache is for the rest of us.

Now the candles were lit. Such radiance, such magnificence, made the tree tremble in all its branches, and one of the candles set fire to the greenery. That stung!

"Dear God!" cried the young ladies and put it out quickly.

Now the tree did not even dare to tremble. Oh, it was awful! It was scared it might lose some of its finery; it was quite dazed by all that brightness. And then the two large doors opened, and a bunch of children came rushing in, looking like they might knock over the tree. The older folks followed more soberly behind. The little ones stood silent, but only for a moment, then their shouts of joy resounded loudly again. They all danced around the tree holding hands and then picked up the gifts one after another.

"What are they doing?" thought the tree. "What's going to happen?" The candles burned all the way down to the branches and, as they burned down, they were put out; and then the children were allowed to take the sweets from the tree. Oh, they rushed in so hard that all the branches groaned; had the top not been tied to the ceiling, the tree would have fallen over.

The children danced about with their magnificent toys. No one looked at the tree except the old nurse, who walked around it as she peeked among the branches, but that was only to see if someone had overlooked a fig or an apple.

"A story! A story!" shouted the children as they pulled a fat little man over toward the tree. He sat down right under it. "For then we are in the green forest," he said, "and the tree can benefit greatly from listening as well! But I'll only tell one story. Do you want the one about 'Ivede-Avede,' or the one about 'Klumpe-

Dumpe,' who fell down the stairs and still ended up on the throne and got the Princess?"

"Ivede-Avede!" shouted some; "Klumpe-Dumpe!" shouted others. There was a lot of yelling and screaming; only the fir tree was quite still and thought, "Am I not part of it? Don't I have anything to do?" But of course it had been part of it and had done what it was supposed to do.

The man then told the story of "Klumpe-Dumpe, who fell down the stairs and still ended up on the throne and got the Princess." And the children clapped their hands and shouted, "More! More!" They also wanted to hear "Ivede-Avede," but they only got the one about "Klumpe-Dumpe." The tree stood completely still and was lost in thought; never had the birds in the forest told it about anything like this. "Klumpe-Dumpe fell down the stairs and still got the Princess! Well, well, that's how it is in the world!" thought the tree, and believed that the story was real, because it was such a nice man who had told it. "Well, well, who knows? Maybe I too shall fall down the stairs and get the Princess." It already looked forward to the next day, to being decorated with candles and toys and gold tinsel and fruits again.

"Tomorrow I won't tremble," it thought. "I will really enjoy myself in all my glory. Tomorrow I shall again hear the story about Klumpe-Dumpe and maybe also the one about Ivede-Avede." The tree stood still and was lost in thought the whole night.

In the morning a manservant and a maid came in.

"Now the decorating begins again," thought the tree. But they dragged it out of the room, up the stairs, and into the loft, where they put it away in a dark corner without any daylight. "What's this about!" thought the tree. "I wonder what I'm supposed to do here. I wonder what I'll get to hear in this place." It leaned up against the wall and stood there, thinking and thinking. It had plenty of time, as days and nights went by. No one came up there, and when someone finally did come, then it was only to put some big boxes over in the corner. The tree was quite hidden, and one would think it was completely forgotten.

"Now it's winter outside," thought the tree. "The ground is hard and covered with snow, and the human beings can't plant me; that's why I have to stand here sheltered until spring. How thoughtful! Human beings are so considerate. If only it weren't so dark and so terribly lonely here. Not even a little hare. It was really lovely out there in the forest, with the snow lying all around and the hare hopping about. Yes, even when it jumped right over me, though I didn't like it then. Up here it's terribly lonely!"

"Peep-peep" said a little mouse just then, as it darted out; and then another little one came. They sniffed at the tree and slipped in and out among its branches.

"It's dreadfully cold!" said the little mice. "Otherwise it's quite lovely here. Don't you think so, old fir tree?"

"I'm not old at all!" said the fir tree. "There are many who are much older than I am."

"Where do you come from," asked the mice, "and what do you know?" They were so awfully curious. "Tell us about the loveliest place on earth. Have you ever been there? Have you been in the larder, where cheeses are lying on the shelves and hams are hanging from the ceiling, where you can dance on tallow candles and go in thin and come out fat?"

"I don't know the larder," said the tree, "but I do know the forest, where the sun shines, and where the birds sing!" Then the tree told everything about its youth. The little mice had never before heard such things. They listened closely and said, "My, how much you've seen! How happy you must have been!"

"I?" said the fir tree and thought about what it had just said. "Yes, they were actually pleasant times!" Then it told about Christmas Eve, when it was decorated with cakes and candles.

"Ooh!" said the little mice, "How happy you've been, you old fir tree."

"I'm not old at all," said the tree, "it's only this winter that I've come in from the forest. I'm in my prime, I've just been temporarily held back in my growth."

"How nicely you tell a story!" said the mice. The next night, they came with four other little mice, who they thought should also hear the tree tell its story. The more it told it, the better it remembered everything, and it thought, "Those were really pleasant times! But they can come again, they can come again. Klumpe-Dumpe fell down the stairs and still got the Princess; maybe I too can get a Princess." Then the fir tree thought about a pretty little birch tree that grew out in the forest; she would be a really lovely Princess for the fir tree.

"Who is Klumpe-Dumpe?" asked the little mice. Then the tree told the whole fairy tale; it could remember every single word. The little mice almost ran up to the top of the tree from sheer delight. In the next nights many more mice came and, on Sunday, even two rats. But the rats said the story was not at all funny. This disappointed the little mice, and now they thought less of it too.

"You only know that one story?" asked the rats.

"Only that one," answered the tree. "I heard it on the happiest night of my life, but at that time I didn't realize how happy I was."

"It's an extremely bad story! Don't you know any about lard and tallow candles? No larder stories?"

"No," said the tree.

"Well then, thanks for nothing," said the rats, and they left.

In the end, the little mice also stayed away. The tree sighed, "It was really quite lovely when those lively little mice sat around me and listened to what I had to say. Now that's also over. But I will remember to enjoy myself when I'm taken out again."

But when was that going to happen? Well! Early one morning people came and moved about in the attic; the boxes were pushed aside, and the tree was dragged out. They threw it onto the hard floor, and right away a manservant dragged it toward the stairs, where the daylight was shining.

"Now life begins again!" thought the tree. It felt the fresh air and the first rays of the sun, and soon it was out in the courtyard. Everything moved very quickly, and the tree completely forgot to look at itself with so much to look at all around it. The yard was right next to a garden, and everything in there was blooming; the roses hung out over the little fence, so fresh and fragrant. The linden trees were blooming, and the swallows flew about and sang, "Kveerra—verra—veet, my husband has arrived!" But it was not the fir tree they meant.

"Now I shall live!" the tree shouted with joy as it spread out its branches. Alas, they were all withered and yellow, and there it lay in a corner among the weeds and the nettles. The gold tinsel star still sat on its top and glittered in the bright sunshine.

In the courtyard a couple of happy children were playing, the ones who at Christmas time had danced around the tree and been so delighted with it. The smallest one rushed over and tore off the gold star.

"Look what's still sitting on that nasty old Christmas tree!" he said as he stomped on the branches, which groaned under his boots.

The tree looked at the wealth of flowers and the freshness in the garden, then it looked at itself, and it wished that it had stayed in its dark corner in the attic. It thought about its fresh youth in the forest, about the merry Christmas Eve, and about the little mice who had been so happy to hear the story of Klumpe-Dumpe.

"It's all over! All over!" said the poor tree. "If I had only enjoyed myself while I could! It's all over! All over!"

The servant came and chopped the tree into little pieces. Pretty soon there was a whole pile lying there, and it made a fine blaze under the big kettle. The tree sighed very deeply, and each sigh was like a little shot. The children who were playing heard it and ran in and sat in front of the fire; they looked into it and shouted, "Bang! Bang!" But with each shot there was a deep sigh, and the tree thought of a summer's day in the forest, or of a winter's night out there, when the stars were shining. It thought of Christmas Eve and of Klumpe-Dumpe, the only fairy tale it had ever heard and knew how to tell. And then the tree was all burned up.

The boys played in the yard, and the smallest one had the gold star on his chest, the same star the tree had worn on the happiest night of its life. Now that night was all over, as it was all over for the tree, and this story is now over too. All over, all over, and so it is with all stories!

THE TALE AT WORK

Like the fir tree, our bodies are often in one place while our minds rush off someplace else. During the workweek we look forward to the weekend, when we plan to relax, have fun, sleep in, and catch up; but by Sunday our minds are already back at work. Or maybe we sit in church or on the beach, but our thoughts are miles away. Or we may be reading the same bedtime story to our kids for the fourth time while thinking about everything that still needs to be done. We pretend to be present, but we are not really there.

I do not advocate that we stop thinking. We need to look back and reflect to avoid repeating the same mistakes, and we need to look ahead and ask "what if" questions for us to grow and create. But asking deep questions is not the same as letting incessant mind chatter take over and rob us of every moment.

Life presents us with the cycle of birth, growth, maturity, decline, decay, and rebirth. Like the cycles of the four seasons and the moon's waxing and waning, something new is always born. Usually we are eager for the first half of the cycle and resist the second. Yet, each has its own gifts. The first offers expansion and excitement, the second deepening and perspective. Within the grand cycle of our life and death, we have many mini-cycles, such as when we develop or lose interest in a relationship, when we begin or drop a hobby, or when we launch or finish a project. We even recognize the cycles when we talk about product life cycles and business cycles.

Unlike the tree, which is severed from its roots, we can stay connected to our essence. If we are doing work that once excited us but now leaves us listless, we can ask ourselves, "Why has the sap stopped flowing, why is there no juice, no zest?" Maybe we have become so pressed by deadlines that we have forgotten why we love what we do? If so, we need to create some space in our life. Or maybe we have outgrown the project? If so, we need to let go, lie fallow for a little while, and allow something new to emerge. All too often, however, instead of taking time to regroup we tend to jump-start the next opportunity. We take advanced placement courses in high school, extra credits in college, and high-visibility projects at work. Always anxious to move on and move up, we cut short our growth.

ANXIOUS TO SHINE

"Oh, . . . if only tonight were here! If only the candles were soon lit! Then what happens? I wonder . . . "

The first half of the story captures the impatience of the modern spirit and the restlessness of the postmodern mind. The tree cannot wait to grow, to get away, and to shine. Bursting with sap and feeling immortal, it is eager to truncate its growth. Yet, because it is so restless and impatient, the tree does not even enjoy the greatest night of its life. Constantly thinking ahead and wondering, "What's next?" it misses its fifteen minutes of fame.

We live in a time with more choices and opportunities than ever before, yet we are less satisfied. Our minds are restless and worry that we may be missing something. We are preoccupied with questions such as, how can we get what we want? How can we fit everything in? How are we measuring up?

Advertising feeds our discontent. We want to wear the new brand, see the blockbuster movie, and taste the microbrewery beer. Like the tree, we are wondering whether there is something "out there" that we are missing. We attend concerts and workshops with a "been there, done that, got the sweatshirt" attitude, and then look around thinking, "Now what?" We become experience addicts, needing the "next new thing" to feel engaged.

In the 1980s people thought it was pretty cool to run a 10K, but now it must be a marathon to get any attention. Having done that, did you run Boston, New York, and Berlin? Did you do the one at Karen Blixen's ranch in Kenya? What about the Great Wall of China? Now that's a real knee breaker! Then what? Maybe a half a triathlon, with an eye on the Iron Man in Hawaii.

Not only do we want to be physically fit, we also want to be a supportive partner, a terrific parent, a top performer, a strong manager, and a visionary leader. Like the little tree, we want to shine. But for whom do we perform? Do we want our parents to be proud of us? Do we try to impress our friends? Do we seek the respect of those who report to us? Kudos from colleagues? A bonus from the boss? In matrixed organizations we try to meet the expectations of various team members and bosses, but barely have we understood their needs before one of us gets reassigned or promoted. The only constant is the demand for greater productivity.

Instead of growing at our own pace, we push. Like the tree, we want to be chosen and given high-visibility projects. We throw ourselves into it, perform beautifully, and before one project is done we have landed two more. When people ask, "how are you?" we answer with a litany of things we have done and what still needs doing. We work through "lunch" and check messages during "breaks," and loved ones become one more to-do, either to be squeezed in or to feel guilty about.

"It is not more time we need: it is fewer desires,"[4] notes Richard Tomkins of the *Financial Times*. In the agrarian society one would grow up and die in the same village. Back then, people could reasonably expect to know everything and do everything that was available to them. Today our "village" is the global workplace and playground. The possibilities are endless, yet we still want to know and do everything. But, as Tomkins observes, "We need to switch off the cell-phone and leave the children to play by themselves. We need to buy less, read less and travel less. We need to set boundaries for ourselves."

But our grasping nature pushes us to behave like brats and demand something more, something new, or something better; until something in us says "enough!" If we do not have the internal fortitude to set limits ourselves, eventually circumstances will do it for us. Things fall through the cracks, tempers get frayed, and the golden boy or girl becomes tarnished. Then we will face a decline in some area of our life, such as in our health, an important relationship, or our career.

BEING CUT DOWN

The ax cut deep into its marrow. The tree fell to the ground with a sigh.

When the tree is stuck in the loft it has time to think, to reflect, and to gain a new perspective on life. But sadly, the tree does not learn. It just becomes nostalgic and resorts to new flights of fancy.

Minor setbacks are common in the workplace, such as the disappointment we feel when we do not measure up. Many of us are only as good as our last quarter's performance; our status goes "up" or "down" with the boss's power; we are "in" or "out" with our market's potential. While we are delighted to be in the spotlight, we become upset when we find ourselves relegated to the "B" team.

Some problems are more serious, even devastating. Like

many, I have had the experience of being laid off, and not surprisingly it felt unfair and unjust. Others see their profession lose prestige or become obsolete, which is painful when you take pride in your line of work. Still others may see a once proud organization go into decline, maybe due to changes in the market or because of incompetent management, and reminisce about the halcyon days. The issue is not that we stumble and fall, the issue is whether we will use our time in "the loft" to reflect, regroup, and learn.

Decline is a tough teacher. It presents us with the choice of becoming a "has-been" or a "seasoned performer." Has-beens spend years nursing their bruised egos and dry up; seasoned performers deepen their roots and grow to their full height. To grow stronger, we need to face our behaviors. Have we taken work so seriously that we have stopped laughing? Have we become a safe bet and lost our edge? Have we treated work as important and child-rearing as mundane? An honest review often hurts, but all experienced "warriors" have at some time been cut to the bone, and they carry the scars to remind them not to make that mistake again.

Though "failure" teaches us some magnificent lessons, we should not invite it needlessly. We can prevent many a decline if we understand what every top-performing athlete knows—stressing the system is necessary, but recovery is also essential. Thus, marathon runners rest before their big events. The strongest riders of the Tour de France ride only a few cycling classics during the spring so they can peak in July. Likewise, we need to understand our own capabilities, both short- and long-term. We need to recognize that it takes time to grow into our full stature. As the motivational speaker Anthony Robbins observes in *Awaken the Giant Within*, "most people overestimate what they can accomplish in a year—and underestimate what they can achieve in a decade!"[5] Just think how the tree, because it was so impatient, lost the opportunity to grow to its full stature as a giant evergreen.

We workplace athletes are pros at producing stress, but we are rookies at recovering. We need to learn to set boundaries, to understand our own rhythms, and to enjoy the ride. We need to stop pushing and start pacing ourselves.

TIME TO THINK

The tree leaned up against the wall and
stood there, thinking and thinking.

We need time to think. I am not suggesting we need more time for the incessant mental distractions that separate us from life, but we do need time to ponder the deeper questions that connect us to it. Instead of automatically adding something to our schedule because it will make us look good, we need to think about whether it is something that also matters. We need to wonder if this is something we care about enough to give it our best energy, our best thinking, our youth, or our remaining years. Will this be fun to do? Will it make life richer? Will it help us grow into the person we want to be?

At Harvard many students are so impatient to shine that they peak before their time. Being aware of this, the dean, Harry R. Lewis, asks freshmen to slow down and get more out of college by doing less. Dean Lewis does not want to discourage achievement, yet he insists that students are more likely to sustain the effort required if they allow time for leisure and solitude. He cautions students not to pack their schedule with so many activities that they have no time to think about *why* they are doing what they are doing. Most precious is their freedom to choose, he insists, which they can maintain only by allowing for unstructured time and flexibility.[6]

Like those ambitious students, many of us schedule ourselves so tightly that we barely have room to breathe. Somehow, we seem to equate busyness with importance and leave no space in our day. Then, needing to be efficient, we tend to skip asking "why" and move straight to "how."

During my time as director of FranklinCovey's one-week executive retreat, held at different mountain resorts, we gave leaders the time to think about their work, leadership, and legacy. The first day participants would often use classroom breaks to call the office, but soon they preferred to watch the light on the mountain and the fish in the stream. The first night they would grab dinner, work, and call home, all while scanning the headlines and responding to messages. But once they settled down, they would hike up to the waterfalls, call home and really talk, or sit by the fire and share their stories—not the well-rehearsed anecdotes to position themselves in the pack, but stories about how they had been wounded and healed, stories about being surprised by joy. By the end of the week they would feel connected to nature, to each other, and to themselves. Their heads had slowed down and their hearts had caught up. They knew what mattered.

But while retreats and reflection help us pay attention, their effect tends to be short-lived, unless every day we find a way to create mini-retreats—a little space to contemplate what is meaningful, what keeps our sap flowing.

A colleague of mine shuts off his phone when commuting and makes time for music. Several clients do not check messages until mid-morning so they can immerse themselves in something important. Some take ten minutes at lunch to reflect on the morning and regroup, rather than rush headlong into the afternoon. Many love walking the dog and taking that time to think about the day. Still others have weekly or quarterly routines. A Canadian attorney told me how she and her husband had been so consumed by their careers and elder care that they had no time for themselves and each other. Being Jewish, however, they had begun to observe the Sabbath, and this time and space for rest, relationships, and religion had become an oasis in their lives. A Swedish manager told me that each quarter, when the business performance had been assessed, he would go for a day-long hike to contemplate his own performance and happiness.

How can you make room for thinking in your life? How can you balance stress and recovery? How can you become less of a human *doing* and more of a human *being*?

CONNECT TO THE CORE

Tomorrow I will really enjoy myself in all my glory.

Like the tree, we are eager to shine. But when we live too much on the periphery, when we are too distracted with the spectacular, we get cut off from our core. Thus we may sip a nice glass of wine but need to look at the label before saying that we like it. To reconnect to your center, you can pay attention to your own stories and the patterns of your life. Do you remember to appreciate what you have while you have it? Are you able to quiet your mind and enjoy life's simple moments? Do you engage wholeheartedly in creative projects? If so, you will draw far more pleasure from life than the wretched little tree.

The tree has a pattern of missing life's simple joys, such as the wind in the face or the cool taste of water. Only when the tree tells the mice about its youth in the forest and they exclaim, "My, how happy you must have been!" does the tree realize that those were indeed wonderful times. Sadly, the tree does not notice how much it is enjoying this very moment with the mice, even as they respond with great enthusiasm to its stories about Christmas Eve and Klumpe-Dumpe.

On the subject of Klumpe-Dumpe, let me digress for a moment. Nearly all the English editions translate the Danish "Klumpe-Dumpe" as "Humpty-Dumpty" to create a near phonetic, though misleading, English translation. In the well-known nursery rhyme, "all the King's horses and all the King's men couldn't put Humpty-Dumpty back together again." Clearly this creature does not get the girl in the end. In contrast, the Klumpe-Dumpe story could be categorized as a "numbskull tale." Such tales usually feature a happy-go-lucky, rather naive hero, who stumbles through events, handles them with aplomb, and ends up with the gold or the princess. Being a rather playful character, such a numbskull would likely have enjoyed the company of the mice and gotten back at the rude rats. A bit of a fool or a trickster, he takes things as they come and reminds us that life is sweet. Sadly, the tree paid attention to the plot instead of the spirit of that tale and began to fantasize about the Princess. Instead of learning the real lesson and enjoying the company of the mice, the tree gets distracted and daydreams about a glorious future. Do we make similar mistakes?

What are your patterns? Do you appreciate what you have, right here, right now? If not, small appreciation rituals can be helpful. A close friend has a two-year-old daughter who, just before going to sleep, goes over the names of every single person she knows. Little Libby created the ritual herself and lingers over each name with a smile, clearly counting her blessings. A more common approach is to keep a journal of gratitude. I love that concept though I have never been able to do it myself.

Recently, however, I heard of a routine that even I can do. A few months ago, the radio program *The Infinite Mind* dealt with "satisfaction," and a researcher presented the latest findings from two studies on the subject. It turns out that people who took just two or three minutes at night to record what they appreciated about their day were markedly more positive, easier to live with, and more likely to exercise. But once a week would not work, it had to be daily.

While it is helpful to think back on the day with appreciation, it is even better to enjoy things right when they happen—the smell of the coffee, the taste of an orange, or the sound of Beethoven's Ninth Symphony. But all too often, as soon as the initial impression is gone, as soon as we have savored the first sips, bites, or bars, we get distracted. To be fully present, we can use the time-tested disciplines of meditation, silence, prayer, yoga, or tai chi to quiet our mind. However, those of us who need it the most are often too restless to stay with it. Even if we think it is valuable, we often find ourselves feeling too busy or too tired to follow through, and instead we collapse in front of the TV for the customary dose of daily programming. But passivity does not bring happiness.

Fortunately, in addition to the meditative practices, there is a very active approach to life right here, right now. One of the most effective ways to be present is to engage in creative projects—something we find worth doing, that stretches us to our limits, that makes us more capable. Parenting is a whopper of a creative project. Many of us also find that running, golfing, singing, painting, or gardening engage our full attention. For a while, one of my "projects" was 100-mile bicycle rides. I would train in the Santa Monica Mountains and push myself as hard as I could, climbing up over the grade and then being fully alert to every rock and pothole as I flew down Mulholland Drive. But then, as soon as it became easy riding along the level Pacific Coast Highway, I would get distracted thinking about the next Century ride or a problem at work. Still, for an extended time I was fully engaged, and I felt completely alive.

Interestingly, people most often report episodes of feeling happy, alive, in a state of "flow" when they are at work, according to Mihaly Csikszentmihalyi, the author of the bestseller *Flow*.

That is because at home we tend to be passive or do routine activities, whereas work gives us more opportunities to do something new, challenging, or creative. We are more likely to experience flow when we cultivate a relationship with our boss that allows us some autonomy, variety, and flexibility. Also, all projects are not created equal. When we choose projects based on what will get the most recognition, we will tend to live on the surface. But if we make our choice based on what is most fulfilling, then we can reach deeper, connect to our roots, and let the energy flow freely.

The difference between living on the surface and being connected to our roots is significant. The tree is always preoccupied, thinking of what might happen or reminiscing about what once was. Also, the tree is always bothered by something, and so it never takes pleasure in life's little joys or relishes its night of glory. Because it never fully lives, its sigh in the end seems tragic. Fortunately, we do not need to make the same mistake. We do not need to waste our attention and energy on what irritates us or on the many reasons to be dissatisfied with life. Instead, we can *engage* with life and *give* ourselves to something we find worth doing. Then our last sigh may be one of deep satisfaction, of knowing we have *lived*.

SOMETHING TO THINK ABOUT . . .

What are your creative projects? What stretches you and helps you develop?

How do you make room for recovery?

SOMETHING TO TALK TO YOUR COLLEAGUES ABOUT . . .

When are we fully engaged; when do we experience a state of flow?

What can we do to allow for more variety, more meaningful challenges, more experimentation in our work?

6

THE NIGHTINGALE

■

When we engage,
we live wholeheartedly.

■

THE NIGHTINGALE delights in life.

With a colorful cast that includes a charming nightingale, a bully of an emperor, a self-important music master, and scurrying courtiers, this story raises two important questions.

What do you value in your work? This question invites us to think about the way we work. Do we tend to respect positional and expert power more than authentic power, to trust reason more than emotion, to value data more than intuition, or to prefer a predictable performance to a splendid and surprising one?

What makes you want to sing your heart out? The issue here is motivation. Most of the characters in the tale are enticed by gold, titles, and applause, so the Emperor bestows favors, golden slippers, and titles. By contrast, the nightingale draws its strength from nature, meaning, intimacy, and freedom—all items outside the Emperor's control. Here lies the key conflict in the tale and in many people's work life.

As you read the following summary or, if you prefer, the full tale, consider these questions: What delights you about the tale? What concerns you? Are you reminded of any nightingales, emperors, and music masters from your work experience?

A SUMMARY OF THE TALE

The Chinese Emperor's palace was made from the most fragile porcelain, and the garden had amazing flowers with little bells tied to them. Everything was very cleverly arranged in the Emperor's realm.

In the forest lived a nightingale who sang so enchantingly that tired laborers were touched by its song. Visitors would write books and poems about the great palace, the garden, and the nightingale.

One day the Emperor was reading one of those books. "But the nightingale is the absolute best!" it was written. "What's this?" shouted the Emperor. He demanded that the nightingale perform at court that very night. If it did not, everyone would be thumped on their bellies right after dinner.

This sent the courtiers scurrying about, for no one at court knew of this bird. Finally they found a little kitchen maid who could lead them to the nightingale. On the way, the courtiers marveled at a cow's mooing and the frog's croaking, mistaking them for the nightingale's song. Finally they saw the plain little bird and extended the Emperor's "invitation."

That night at the palace the nightingale sang so beautifully that tears rolled down the Emperor's cheeks. The Emperor was so moved he wanted to hang his golden slipper around its neck. But the nightingale declined, saying the Emperor's tears were the best reward.

The Emperor insisted the nightingale stay at court. So the

little bird was "given" a golden cage and twelve servants to watch over it, plus the "liberty" to walk outside a couple of times a day.

After some time, a gift arrived: It was an artificial nightingale, made of gold and precious gems. It could sing the exact same piece thirty-three times without getting tired and was an instant success. Meanwhile, the live nightingale escaped out the open window. Furious, the Emperor banished the bird from his realm.

The Music Master then assured everyone that they still had the best bird, and everyone agreed. The mechanical nightingale was given the place of honor on the Emperor's night table. But one evening, as it was singing, something inside it snapped and the music stopped. The watchmaker repaired the bird, but it could be played only sparingly.

Five years passed and the Emperor was lying alone on his deathbed. A new Emperor had already been chosen and everyone had run out to greet him. The old Emperor could scarcely breathe because Death was sitting on his chest. All around the bed strange faces appeared, their soft voices recounting the Emperor's good and evil deeds. Tormented, the Emperor cried for the golden bird to sing, but there was no one there to wind it up.

Suddenly the loveliest song came from right outside the window. The real nightingale had responded to the Emperor's distress and had come to comfort him. Gradually, the strange faces faded away, Death drifted out the window, and the Emperor got a good night's sleep.

In the morning the Emperor asked the nightingale to stay at the palace. The nightingale declined, but it promised to come each evening and sing for the Emperor so that he might be both joyful and thoughtful. Then it flew away.

Shortly after the servants came to take a look at their dead Emperor. Imagine their surprise when they found him completely recovered: Well, there they stood. And the Emperor said: "Good morning"!

DID YOU KNOW . . . Two events inspired

The Nightingale: the opening of Tivoli Gardens in Copenhagen and meeting the great singer Jenny Lind, in her time called the Swedish Nightingale.

In August 1843, Tivoli Gardens had just opened. It was a magical place with Chinese pagodas, colored lanterns, peacocks, fireworks, lakes, flowers, restaurants, theaters, and amusement rides. The next month, H. C. Andersen met Jenny Lind when she first performed in Copenhagen. She was later to become the toast of Vienna, have tea with Queen Victoria in London, and tour the United States.

At first H. C. Andersen thought Lind to be extremely plain, but when he heard her sing he was captivated and fell deeply in love. As a true romantic, however, he seemed to prefer the feeling of being in love to having an adult love relationship; thus, even when he proposed to Lind by letter, he made sure to mention several reasons why she might not find him eligible. Lind, however, was never romantically interested in the writer, but always thought of him as a brother.

The Nightingale was written in an amazing burst of creativity. H. C. Andersen noted in his journal on October 11, 1843: "In Tivoli Gardens. Started the Chinese fairy tale." Already the very next night he wrote, "Dined at home, visited, finished the Chinese tale."

H. C. Andersen rarely included *The Nightingale* in his readings. But from his correspondence we know that he gave a reading of it in 1852 during one of his frequent visits to Weimar, Germany, and that it was the composer Franz Liszt's favorite tale.

THE CLASSIC TALE

IN CHINA, AS YOU KNOW, the Emperor is Chinese, and all those around him are Chinese too. This story happened many years ago, but that is precisely why it is worth telling it before we forget it. The Emperor's palace was the most splendid in the world, made entirely and completely from fine porcelain that was precious, but so fragile that one had to be very careful when touching it. In the garden were the most amazing flowers, and next to the most beautiful ones were tied silver bells that rang, so that one could not walk by them without paying attention. Yes, everything was so cleverly arranged in the Emperor's garden.

The garden stretched so far that even the gardener did not know the end of it. If you continued to walk, you came to the most beautiful forest with tall trees and deep lakes. The forest went straight down to the sea, which was blue and deep, so large ships could sail right in underneath the branches. In these branches lived a nightingale that sang so sweetly that even the poorest fisherman, who had so much to attend to, would stop and listen when he was out at night pulling up his nets and heard the nightingale. "Dear Lord, how beautiful it is!" he said. But then he had to tend to things and forgot about the bird. Still the next night, when the nightingale sang again and the fisherman came out, he said the same thing: "Dear Lord! How very beautiful it is!"

From all the countries in the world, travelers came to the Emperor's city, and they admired it—the city, the palace, and the garden. But when they heard the nightingale, they all said the same thing: "This is the very best!"

The travelers spoke about it when they returned home, and the learned wrote many books about the city, the palace, and the garden. But they never forgot about the nightingale—it was at the very top of the list. And those who could write poetry wrote such beautiful poems, all of them about the nightingale in the forest by the deep sea.

The books made it around the world and some even made it back to the Emperor. He sat on his golden throne, and read and read. He nodded his head all the time, because he so enjoyed hearing the magnificent descriptions of his city, palace, and garden. "But the nightingale is the very best!" it was written.

"What's this?" said the Emperor, "The nightingale! But I don't know it at all! Is there such a bird in my empire? On top of that, in my own garden? I have never heard that! One has to read about such!"

And then he called his chamberlain, who was so distinguished that when anyone of lower rank dared to talk to him or ask him anything, he only answered "P!"—and that meant nothing at all.

"There's supposed to be a most remarkable bird here called nightingale!" said the Emperor. "It is said to be the very best thing in my great empire! Why hasn't anyone ever told me anything about it?"

"I have never heard it mentioned before!" said the chamberlain. "It has never been presented at court!"

"It must come here tonight and sing for me," said the Emperor. "Here the whole world knows what I have, and I don't know it!"

"I have never heard it mentioned before," said the chamberlain, "but I shall look for it, and I shall find it!"

But where was it to be found? The chamberlain ran up and down all the stairs, through all the halls and corridors, but no one among the many he ran into had heard talk of the nightingale. And the chamberlain ran to the Emperor once more and said that this was likely a fable—created by those who write books. "Your Imperial Majesty must not believe everything that is written! It is all made up, something called the black art!"

"But the book in which I read it," said the Emperor, "was sent to me by the Mighty Emperor of Japan, so it cannot be untrue. I will hear the nightingale! It shall be here tonight! I shall grant it my highest favor! And if it doesn't come, then the whole court shall be thumped on their bellies right after they have eaten their dinner!"

"Tsing-pe!" said the chamberlain, and once more ran up and down all the stairs through all the halls and corridors; and half the court ran along, for they did not want to be thumped on their bellies! They all asked about the remarkable nightingale the whole world, but no one at court, knew about.

Finally they came upon a poor little girl in the kitchen, who said, "Dear God, the nightingale! I know it well! Yes, how it can sing! Every night I'm permitted to take a few leftovers and bring them home to my poor sick mother, who lives down by the shore. And when I walk back and get tired and rest in the forest, then I hear the nightingale sing. It brings tears to my eyes; it's just as if my mother were kissing me."

The chamberlain declared, "The little kitchen maid shall be provided with a permanent position in the kitchen and permission to watch the Emperor eat, if she will lead us to the nightingale, for it has been summoned for tonight."

And then they all set out for the forest where the nightingale usually sang, and half of the court came along. As they walked along, a cow started mooing.

"Oh!" said the courtiers. "Here we have it. It's really an unusual force for such a little creature. I have most certainly heard it before."

"No, that's the cows that are mooing," said the little kitchen maid. "We're still far from the place."

Then the frogs started to croak in the pond.

"Wonderful!" said the palace chaplain, "Now I hear it. It's like little church bells!"

"No, that's the frogs!" said the little kitchen maid. "But now, I think we'll soon hear it."

Then the nightingale began to sing.

"That's it!" said the little girl. "Listen! Listen! There it is!" And then she pointed to a little gray bird up in the branches.

"Is that possible?" said the chamberlain. "I had never thought it would look like that! How plain it looks! It must have lost its color by having so many prominent people come visit."

"Little nightingale," shouted the little kitchen maid quite loudly, "our gracious Emperor would so very much like you to sing for him!"

"With the greatest pleasure," said the nightingale, and it sang most delightfully.

"It is just like glass bells!" said the chamberlain. "And look at the tiny throat. How it uses it! It is strange that we have never heard it before. It will be a great success at court."

"Shall I sing for the Emperor again?" asked the nightingale, who thought the Emperor had come along.

"My splendid little nightingale," said the chamberlain, "I have the great pleasure to summon you to the court celebration tonight where you will enchant his High Imperial Eminence with your charmante song!"

"It sounds best outdoors, in the green wood," said the nightingale, but it gladly came along when it heard that the Emperor wanted it.

At the palace, everything had been properly polished. The

walls and floors made from porcelain glowed to the light of thousands of golden lamps. The most wonderful flowers, which actually could tinkle, were placed along the corridors. And there was such a running about that with the draft all the bells tinkled, so you could not hear yourself think.

In the middle of the great hall, where the Emperor was sitting, was a golden perch, where the nightingale was to sit. The whole court was there, and the little kitchen maid had been given permission to stand behind the door, since she now had the title of "real kitchen maid." Everyone was wearing their greatest finery. And everyone looked at the little gray bird, and the Emperor nodded at it.

The nightingale sang so beautifully that the Emperor got tears in his eyes, and the tears rolled down his cheeks. And then the nightingale sang even more beautifully! It went straight to the heart. The Emperor was most delighted, and he said that the nightingale was to have his golden slipper to wear around its neck. But the nightingale said no, thank you; it had already been rewarded enough.

"I have seen tears in the Emperor's eyes, and that is the richest treasure! An Emperor's tears have a strange power. God knows I have been rewarded!" And then it sang once more with its sweet blessed voice.

"This is the most adorable coquetterie I know," said the ladies all around. And then they put water in their mouth so they could warble when someone talked to them, for they thought they were nightingales too. Even the footmen and the chambermaids let it be known that they were content, and that is saying a lot, for they are the most difficult to please. Yes, the nightingale was certainly a success!

It was now to remain at court, have its own cage, plus the liberty to go for a walk twice during the day and once at night. It was given twelve servants to bring along. Each of them had a silk ribbon tied around one of its legs, and held on to it tightly. There was no pleasure at all in that walk.

The whole city talked about the amazing bird. When two people met each other, one of them would say only "Night!" and the other "Gale!" and then they would sigh and understand each other. Yes, and eleven butchers' children were named after it, though not one of them could carry a tune!

One day the Emperor received a large package. On the outside was written Nightingale.

"Here's another new book about our famous bird!" said the Emperor. But it was not a book, it was a small work of art that was lying in a box—an artificial nightingale, made to look like the real one, except it was covered with diamonds, rubies, and sapphires! As soon as the artificial bird was wound up, it could sing one of the melodies the real one sang, and then its tail went up and down, gleaming with silver and gold. Around its neck was a small ribbon, and on it was written, "The Japanese Emperor's nightingale is cheap compared to the Emperor of China's."

"It's lovely!" they all said. And the person who had brought the artificial bird was promptly given the title of "high-imperial-nightingale-bringer."

"Now they must sing together. What a duet that will be!"

So they had to sing together, but that didn't go so well, for the real nightingale sang in its own way, and the artificial bird went on automatic rollers.

"That's not its fault," said the Music Master about the artificial bird. "It keeps perfect time and is in line with my system." The artificial bird was then to sing by itself. It was just as much of a success as the real one, and it was so much more lovely to look at, as it sparkled like bracelets and brooches.

Thirty-three times it sang one and the same melody, and it still wasn't tired. People would gladly have listened to it from the beginning again, but the Emperor thought that now the living nightingale should also sing a little. But where was it? No one had noticed that it had flown out the open window and gone away to its green forests.

"But what's this?" said the Emperor. And all the courtiers scolded the nightingale and thought that it was a most ungrateful creature.

"We still have the best bird," they said, and then the artificial bird had to sing again. That was the thirty-fourth time they got the same tune, but they still did not know it by heart because it was so intricate. And the Music Master praised the bird highly and assured everyone that it was better than the real nightingale, not only because of the way it was dressed and the many lovely diamonds, but also on the inside.

"For you see, ladies and gentlemen, and above all your Imperial Highness, with the real nightingale one can never calculate what will happen, what will come next, but with the artificial bird everything is determined. So it will be and no differently! One can account for it, one can cut it open and show the human thinking, how the music rollers lie, how they move, and how one thing follows the next."

"That's precisely what I think," they all said. And, on the following Sunday, the Music Master was permitted to show the bird to the people, for they should also hear it sing, said the Emperor. And they heard it, and they were just as delighted as if they had all drunk themselves merry with tea water, for that is so very Chinese. And everyone then said "Oh!" and stuck the finger we call the index finger high in the air, and then they nodded. But the poor fisherman, who had heard the real nightingale, said: "It sounds beautiful enough, it also looks like it, but something is missing. I don't know what!"

And the real nightingale was banished from the realm.

The artificial bird now had its place on the silk cushion close to the Emperor's bed. All the gifts it had received, gold and gems, were lying around it. In title it had risen to "high-imperial-bedside-table-singer." In rank, it was number one on the left side, for the Emperor considered that to be the most distinguished side because that is where the heart is, and the heart is also on the left side in the Emperor. The Music Master wrote twenty-five volumes about the artificial bird, which were very learned and very long and used all the most difficult Chinese words. Everyone said that they had read and understood them, for otherwise they would have been considered stupid and then they would have been thumped on their bellies.

And so it went for a whole year. The Emperor, the court, and all the other Chinese knew by heart every "cluck" that the artificial bird sang. But that was precisely why they liked it the very best. They could sing along, and that they did. Street urchins sang "Zizizi! Cluck-cluck-cluck!" and the Emperor sang it! Yes, it was so very lovely!

But one evening, as the artificial bird was singing and the Emperor was lying in bed listening to it, the bird went "Boing!" inside. Something popped. "Whirrrrrrrrr!" All the wheels spun around, and the music stopped.

The Emperor leaped out of bed and had his personal physician summoned. But what good was that! Then they had the watchmaker fetched, and after much talking and much looking, he more or less put the bird back together again. But he said that the bird had to be played sparingly, for the cogs were very worn and it was not possible to replace them in a way that the music could be guaranteed. That was terribly sad! Only once a year did they dare let the artificial bird sing, and even that was hard enough. But then the Music Master gave a little speech with all the difficult words and said that it was just as good as before—and so it was as good as before.

Now five years had passed, and the whole country suffered a really great sorrow because, after all, they were all fond of their

Emperor, who was sick and would not live, it was said. A new Emperor had already been chosen, but the people stood in the street and asked the chamberlain how it was with their Emperor.

"P!" he said, and shook his head.

Cold and pale, the Emperor lay in his great, magnificent bed. The whole court thought him dead and all of them had run over to greet the new Emperor. The footmen ran out to talk about it, and the chambermaids had a big coffee klatch. In all the halls and corridors cloth had been put down so one would not hear people walk, and it was so quiet, so very quiet. But the Emperor was not yet dead. Stiff and pale, he lay in his magnificent bed with the long velvet curtains and the heavy golden tassels. High up, a window was open, and the moon was shining in on the Emperor and the artificial bird.

The poor Emperor could hardly breathe. It was as if something were sitting on his chest. He opened his eyes, and then he saw that it was Death who was sitting on his chest. It had put on his golden crown, and in one hand it held the Emperor's saber and in the other his magnificent banner. And around him, in the folds of the great velvet curtains, the most unusual faces peered forth, some of them quite hideous and others so blessedly mild: These were all the Emperor's evil and good deeds looking at him, now that Death was sitting on his heart.

"Do you remember that?" they whispered one after the other. "Do you remember that?" And then they told him so much that the sweat poured from his forehead.

"I never knew that!" said the Emperor. "Music, music! The great Chinese drums!" he shouted, "so I don't have to hear what they're saying!"

Still they continued, and Death nodded, in the way the Chinese do, at everything that was said.

"Music, music!" cried the Emperor. "You blessed little golden bird, sing! Sing! I have given you gold and treasures. I personally put my golden slipper around your neck. Do sing! Sing!"

But the bird stood still. There was no one there to wind it, so it could not sing. Meanwhile Death, with its big empty eye sockets, continued to look at the Emperor, and it was so quiet, so dreadfully quiet!

At that very moment the loveliest song sounded near the window. It was the real little nightingale sitting on a branch outside. It had heard of the Emperor's need and had come to sing him comfort and hope. And as it sang, the faces in the curtain became paler and paler. The blood came faster and faster to the Emperor's weak limbs. And Death itself listened and said, "Continue, little nightingale, continue!"

"Yes, if you give me the magnificent golden saber! Yes, if you give me the great banner! Yes, if you give me the Emperor's crown!"

And Death gave each treasure for a song. And the nightingale continued to sing. It sang about the quiet churchyard where the white roses grow, where the elderberries scent the air, and where the fresh grass is watered by the tears of the bereaved. Then Death began to long for its garden and drifted like a cold white mist out the window.

"Thank you, thank you!" said the Emperor. "You heavenly little bird, I know you well. I drove you from my realm, and still you have sung the evil visions away from my bed, and removed Death from my heart! How can I reward you?"

"You have rewarded me!" said the nightingale. "You gave me your tears the first time I sang for you. I'll never forget it. They are the jewels that touch a singer's heart. But sleep now and get well and strong! I'll sing for you."

And it sang—and the Emperor fell into a sweet sleep, a gentle and restorative sleep.

The sun was shining on him through the window when he

awoke, strengthened and healthy. None of his servants had returned, for they thought he was dead. But the nightingale still sat there singing.

"You must always stay with me," said the Emperor, "You shall only sing when you want to, and I will break the artificial bird into a thousand pieces."

"Don't do that!" said the nightingale. "It has done the good it could. Keep it as always. I cannot build my nest and live at the palace, but let me come to you when I feel like it. Then I shall come in the evening and sit on the branch by the window and sing for you, so you may be joyful—and thoughtful. And I shall sing of those who are happy and of those who suffer. I shall sing of the evil and the good that is kept hidden from you. The little songbird flies far and wide: to the poor fisherman, to the farmer's roof, to everyone who is far from you and your court. I love your heart more than your crown, although the crown does have a scent of something holy about it. I shall come and sing for you. Only you must promise me one thing."

"Anything!" said the Emperor. He stood in his imperial robe, which he had put on by himself, and held his heavy gold saber up to his heart.

"Only one thing I ask of you. Don't tell anyone that you have a little bird who tells you everything; then everything will be even better."

Then the nightingale flew away.

When at last the servants came to take a look at their dead Emperor, well, there they stood. And the Emperor said, "Good morning!"

THE TALE AT WORK

The nightingale's song represents the genuine life force in each of us, our essence, our central way of being, our inherent talent and passion, our special brand of energy, our authentic power. Such energy cannot be boosted by fake stimulants like coffee, sugar, popularity, pep talks, or perks, nor is it squandered on trivial activities. Instead, it thrives on meaningful challenges, genuine participation, and wholehearted contributions.

The raw voice of Billie Holiday is a great example of authentic power. Her talent was so strong that her limited vocal abilities became irrelevant. At first, producers gave her second-rate songs to record, but she breathed such life into those lyrics and melodies that she soon received great material. Today we may hear her voice as we rush through a store or grab lunch at a café, and, like the busy fisherman in *The Nightingale*, we are touched by her song. Although Billie Holiday's life was in many ways heartbreaking, it was *her* life, her special way of being in the world.

But not all famous artists, athletes, scientists, professionals, or businesspeople give of themselves like Billie Holiday. Instead, many use their knowledge and talent in a calculated manner. Such efforts are like the mechanical nightingale: beautiful, sparkling, and satisfying on the surface, but they make no deep or genuine connection.

Like such artists, we may be stingy or generous with our talent. Most people feel pressured to perform, continuously cut costs, and increase productivity. As a result, because of overload or resentment, we give a perfunctory performance. We forget our responsibility to our own potential.

Fortunately, we can make a different choice. In this chapter we will be inspired by the little nightingale to develop our potential and engage wholeheartedly. Some may consider this an idealistic approach to life. Good, because the world needs idealists. What is more, this does not mean we have to give up being realistic; the nightingale is neither clueless nor naive about human nature.

We will look also at the forces that seek to suppress the vibrancy and vitality of life. These include positional power, as symbolized by the Emperor, and expert power, exemplified by the Music Master. These are tendencies that are inside all of us and therefore are reflected in our workplaces. Finally, we will be encouraged to offset positional and expert power with authentic power, which we will be able to do when we connect to our essence and commit to our unique way of being.

THE NIGHTINGALE AS A MODEL

. . . a nightingale that sang so sweetly that even the poorest fisherman, who had so much to attend to, would stop and listen . . .

How might you tap into your authentic power and share of yourself? *The Nightingale* shows the way. Sing as often you can, do not get your feathers ruffled, connect to your source of power, and sing your heart out.

Sing as Often as You Can

The nightingale loves to sing. It sings every day and refreshes the tired fisherman and the Emperor alike. Over time, it develops mastery. When the Emperor is moved to tears, it sings even more sweetly. When Death sits on the Emperor's chest, the little bird's song is so strong that it can even negotiate with Death. Does your work energize you? Do you enjoy the way you do the work? Do the people you work with bring out the best in you?

Sam Cohen, a concentration camp survivor, spent forty-six years behind the deli counter at Zabar's, my favorite New York deli. By working sixty-hour weeks he put his daughter though dental school and his son through medical school. Sam Cohen delighted people with his "song." Not only was he an acclaimed master of salmon slicing, he was also a man who flirted shamelessly with the women and who greeted the men as friends. He always looked to create a joyous life for everyone around the counter.

Do Not Get Your Feathers Ruffled

Most people in the tale do not recognize the nightingale's talent, but go along with what is popular or what the experts say. They cannot tell the lovely melody from a frog's croaking, or real talent from a well-packaged performance. Still, the nightingale does not whine and complain that it is being misunderstood; it simply continues to sing. Do you feel undervalued and underpaid or trapped by a soft labor market? If so, are you spending your time whining, or rather developing professional mastery?

The twentieth-century Spanish composer Joaquin Rodrigo had a rough start in life. He lost his sight as a child and was a refugee during the Spanish Civil War, but even so he stayed dedicated to his music. Rodrigo wanted to make Spanish music, but not the "españolada" (patriotic *pasodobles*) the public enjoyed. He wanted to make modern music, but not the avant-garde music the critics praised. So people found his classical compositions too serious, and the critics dismissed them as easy listening. But Rodrigo did not get his feathers ruffled, he just said, "My cup may be small, but it is from my own cup that I drink."[1] He was a modest man who produced masterpieces like the *"Concierto de Aranjuez"* for guitar and was recognized with more international prizes and honors than any other Spanish composer.

Connect to Your Source of Power

While the nightingale is pleasant, it is not a pushover. Though everyone else scurries to satisfy the Emperor's every whim, the little bird declines his golden slipper, leaves the palace, and refuses to return. Not because it is selfish and stingy, but because it needs to be nourished by the forest and freedom before it can refresh others. Only by staying connected to its source of energy can it remain strong. What distracts and drains you? What focuses and nourishes you? To what should you be saying "no"?

Many businesspeople and athletes are energized by competition. In the 1980s the Lakers and the Celtics were the reigning basketball dynasties and Magic Johnson and Larry Bird led their respective teams in the showdowns. Both thrived on the rivalry and played their hearts out. They baited each other in pregame interviews, yet they clearly respected each other. Magic knew that a great opponent is a source of energy and often said that Bird made him a better player.

Sing Your Heart Out

The nightingale does not respond to the usual carrot and stick approach, such as gold, titles, or being beaten on the belly. Instead, it wants freedom, intimacy (the Emperor's tears), and meaning. Because it understands the source of its power, it always gives a great performance. What makes you want to sing your heart out?

Carolyn Curtis was one person whose song inspired me. For years I led an executive leadership retreat at Sundance, Robert Redford's mountain resort in Utah, and Carolyn was the program coordinator. At the end of the week, we hotshot program leaders would get 9s and 10s on our evaluations, but participants would time and again expand the scale to an 11 or 12 for Carolyn. She connected with them, anticipated their needs, and created a home away from home. Carolyn did not do it for the money or career opportunities, not even for the peer recognition. In fact, while the customers loved her, most people inside the firm did not hear how special her song was. She did it because she was passionate about the work and cared about the people who attended the programs.

Like the nightingale, we can delight others with our work when we understand the difference between giving of our time and giving of ourselves, between working hard and working wholeheartedly.

To be remarkable, however, we must also be resilient. We must have the strength to engage with powerful emperors and elitist music masters who consider nightingales disruptive.

THE EMPEROR AND THE MUSIC MASTER

. . . then the artificial bird had to sing again.
That was the thirty-fourth time they got the same tune, . . .

Many emperors and music masters think nightingales are difficult to manage, because their essence, their central way of being, does not respond predictably to pay, perks, and popularity. While an impressive performance may be good, they believe that repeatable and reliable results are even better.

In publicly traded companies, a predictable quarterly performance is essential. Like the absolute monarchs in H. C. Andersen's time, today's analysts, shareholders, and boards have no tolerance for surprises. CEOs must give accurate forecasts or they lose their credibility, managers must hit financial targets or they lose their bonuses, and individuals must meet productivity targets or they lose their jobs. As the saying goes, it is nothing personal, just business. To avoid such unpleasantness, we accept leaving people in charge who behave like emperors and music masters. We then keep our nightingale quiet by numbing it with drinks, happy pills, workaholism, or too much TV. On the surface, it seems like a small price to pay.

While we can easily spot the emperors and music masters in others, it is our inner ones we need to be aware of the most.

Within each of us, the emperor represents our ambitious and driven self, the part of us that pays attention to our own and other people's place in the hierarchy, the one that understands power. This character can read the office politics and figure out how to influence people. Although our inner emperor can get us in trouble if we cut him loose, he can also accomplish many good things for us. He can help us build a marketable portfolio, strategize to get the position we want, and negotiate some flexibility.

We also possess a music master, which is our analytical mind, our need to see the data and hard evidence before we act. Our inside music master trusts things that can be observed, quantified, and tracked. He is organized, disciplined, and efficient. As long as this character does not become too dominant, repeatedly disregarding our feelings and intuition, he can be a great help in getting the job done.

These forces for control and predictability are inside of us and consequently are reflected in our workplaces. Emperors rule hierarchical structures and music masters manage productivity.

Let us take a look at these characters in turn to see how they may help or hinder genuine engagement. Depending on how they act in your workplace, your situation may be healthy, harmful, or promising.

"EMPERORS" AT WORK

. . . if the nightingale doesn't come, then the whole court shall be thumped on their bellies, right after they have eaten their dinner!

Hierarchies create emperors at all levels. Though much maligned, hierarchical structures are remarkably resilient as a way to organize and gain status. Even if we resent their undemocratic nature, we like to use position and access as a way to keep score.

In our tale, the Emperor uses both subtle and heavy-handed means of control. The palace and gardens showcase the Emperor's authority, just as today's executive corridors convey power. In such places children would know immediately that their exuberance will be suppressed, and that laughter, skipping, or playing will be discouraged. Adults recognize this as well, but are seduced by the display of wealth and the proximity to power.

The Emperor wants to add the nightingale to his possessions. Usually, golden slippers, gems, or titles would close such a deal, but the nightingale does not respond as expected. Instead, it wants intimacy (the genuine connection shown by the Emperor's tears) and freedom. The nightingale seemingly wants very little, yet it is too much for the Emperor to give; he cannot relinquish control.

Therefore, the Emperor resorts next to the heavy-duty power tool of coercion. But he wants to keep up the pretense of voluntary participation, so he *lets* the nightingale have its own cage plus the *liberty* to stroll outside, and *gives* it twelve servants to bring along. Even with this tactic, the Emperor's aim still is to capture the bird's life force. But as Margaret Wheatley, an expert on natural systems, says, "You can't boss life around." Not surprisingly, the minute the Emperor is distracted, the nightingale escapes out the window and reclaims its freedom.

Later in the tale the courtiers also leave, but for the opposite reason. The Emperor has lost his grip on power and a new ruler has been selected. Since the courtiers' self-worth is connected to their position, the old ruler is now a liability, and they leave to curry favor with the new boss.

In the end, the Emperor is completely alone. Facing Death, he is tormented by regrets, and he cries for relief. The little nightingale responds, bringing him comfort with its song. After a restful and restorative night's sleep, the Emperor awakens to a new sense of responsibility. We have the promise of a new day—one where the Emperor, instead of serving his own ego, will serve for the good of the realm. For those attached to positional power, however, such a change is problematic. As the servants come to take a look at their dead Emperor, his "Good Morning" sounds more unsettling than promising.

Consider the dominant players in your workplace. Do they look out for "number one" instead of the good of the organization? Do they rely on golden slippers and belly beatings, the carrot-and-stick approach, to motivate people? Do they seek to control or exploit people's energy, and disguise their intentions with management jargon? If so, do not be naive and expect them to change. Be street-smart and look at your options. Is your best choice to speak up, transfer, or leave? You do not have to act immediately, or perhaps at all, just do not allow yourself to be deceived.

Hopefully, your boss and other key players value your talent and use their power for the good of the organization. If that is the case, do not be stingy. Be generous with your time and energy, stretch to 100 percent of your abilities, and give your best performance.

"MUSIC MASTERS" AT WORK

But the artificial bird stood still.
There was no one to wind it, so it could not sing.

H. C. Andersen offers a perceptive description of the analytical mind when the Music Master addresses the court: "For you see, ladies and gentlemen, and above all, your Imperial Highness, with the real nightingale one can never calculate what will happen, what will come next, but with the artificial bird everything is determined. So it will be and no differently! One can account for it, one can cut it open and show the human thinking, how the music rollers lie, how they move, and how one thing follows the next."

Such thinking shaped our modern industrial corporations, where decisions were based on data and favored efficiency, productivity, and progress. Today H. C. Andersen would likely have made the Music Master a high-priced consultant, an impressive productivity expert with a business bestseller to his name, someone to whom corporate emperors would defer.

Frederick W. Taylor was the dominant music master of the twentieth century. His method of *scientific management* created breakthrough efficiencies on the factory floor. Later, Alfred Sloan, CEO of General Motors, brought analytical thinking to the front office. To him, people who made good decisions were the "raw material" of management, and good decisions were "completely fact-based and purged of all personal concerns." In fact, the worst Sloan could say about a manager was that he allowed personal considerations to enter into his business decisions.[2] A century after Taylor, the cult of efficiency continues to thrive. Most of us have been merged, reorganized, or reengineered, all in the service of ever-greater productivity. Of course, it is because of these amazing advances in productivity that we enjoy a very high standard of living.

The music-master mentality also helps create merit-based workplaces. In an attempt to be objective and to pay people based on performance, we identify roles, define competencies, establish metrics, and track progress.

But sometimes, in our aim to be fair, we treat people as objects. We prescribe processes and send in mystery shoppers to evaluate the results: Do employees give eye contact, say "welcome" with a smile, and greet the customer by name? While these efforts may guarantee a minimum standard, the joy Sam Cohen created around him at Zabar's deli counter is not something that can be measured. Unfortunately, because such special qualities cannot be counted, they are often discounted.

Music masters can be discouraging bosses for people who are spectacular and surprising in their performance. On the other hand, they can be good managers for people who like clear rules and are turned on by efficiencies.

Most often, the reason the quality of our work life suffers is a strained relationship with our boss or some other key player. Hoping they will change is wishful thinking, however. The more practical choice is for us to take responsibility for the relationship ourselves. Fortunately, in my coaching of leaders, I have seen many problematic relationships improve and become productive when one party stops getting his or her feathers ruffled and pays attention to the other person's (often quite legitimate) needs.

As we have seen, emperors and music masters can be formidable characters, but to successfully deal with them we need to see them as they are. Then we have a choice, either to engage or disengage.

More important, we need to face our inner emperor, our inner music master, and sometimes also an unassertive nightingale. The next section shows how we can remain alert to these characters' presence and keep them from running our life.

AUTHENTIC POWER AT WORK

But when they heard the nightingale,
they all said the same thing: "This is the very best!"

Compared to our parents and grandparents, we have an astonishing array of opportunities and options in life. Our challenge is not to choose what matters over what does not matter, but to decide what matters most. Except that, being on the fast track, we have become impatient with the slower and more thoughtful parts of ourselves.

To tap into our deepest source of power, we need to slow down and reflect. Let me discuss just three things worth thinking about. We need to be able to tell an adrenaline rush from authentic energy, a status-based high from real power, and wishful thinking from genuine passion and commitment.*

Many of us are distracted by urgencies, addicted to urgencies, and even mistake urgencies for importance. If you have a pattern of sixty-hour workweeks, if you are constantly driven by deadlines, if you are fast-paced and impatient, then you are at risk! Hit the pause button and give yourself some time to relax and reflect. Ask yourself, "Is it the tough deadlines, the adrenaline, and the caffeine that gives me a rush, or is it the work itself that makes me want to get out of bed in the morning?"

At one of my retreats, an executive was considering his work-life balance. Having been asked to write down what he would like others to say at his memorial service, this man actually called his wife and surprised her with the question, "Hi dear, if I were dead what would you say about me?" Taken aback, her immediate answer was, "Well, you are a hard worker . . ." Granted, he worked seventy-hour weeks, but that these were the first words out of her mouth shook him. So, he interrupted her, "That's what you'd say about me?" Apparently, she quickly recovered and gave the standard answers about being a wonderful father and a loving husband. Fortunately, he was already bothered.

We are often seduced by high-paying, high-status jobs. Let us say you get an offer to be part of a prestigious project, where the

*If you would like a complimentary copy of "Essentials for Self-Leadership," please go to www.mettenorgaard.com.

pay is great and a promotion possible, in other words, quite a status kick. Yet, the project will take months to complete and require a move. Your inner emperor and music master agree that this is a practical move, and you head home to persuade the family. At such times, however, you need to pause long enough to consider whether the move is likely to make you genuinely strong. Listen to the nightingale's voice: "Does the assignment itself intrigue me? Will the project be able to sustain my interest for months? Do I respect the people I will work with? Is it really worth the price that loved ones will have to pay?"[3]

We also need to distinguish between wishful thinking and real passion. Many believe that to be happy we must quit work and write the great American novel, start our own restaurant, or join the Peace Corps. For a few people this may be their vocation, but for most it is a fantasy, a case of seeking work-life happiness in a make-believe scenario, instead of in our own passion and commitment.

To sort fantasy from facts, the no-nonsense radio psychologist David Viscott used to give the following advice. When callers complained they were unhappy and wanted to quit work and become writers, Viscott would ask, "How much are you writing now?" If they griped, "I don't have time to write now," he would tell them to get started. Viscott would suggest they write every day, write on weekends, write during vacations, simply write, write, write. Then, once they needed more time to write, they might drop to half-time employment. Only when all that time was consumed by writing should they consider quitting. Looking to one's own behavior is an excellent way to test one's commitment.

Unfortunately, when it comes to our dreams, Disney's Jiminy Cricket misleads us when he croons, "When you wish upon a star . . . ," and suggests that wishing alone will make our dreams come true. Dr. Freeman Hrabowski, president of the University of Maryland, did more than dream; he had what it took to make it happen. At the age of thirteen he visited the Tuskegee Institute, and there he was inspired to make science his life. He began to see himself as having a Ph.D., teaching math, and being a dean. To reinforce his vision, the teenager had a great routine. Every morning he would look into the mirror and say, "Good morning, Dr. Hrabowski." The vision was clear, and he also had the commitment to make it happen.

The choreographer Twyla Tharp says in her book *The Creative Habit* that making our dreams a reality requires an "insane" commitment. Even at the age of sixty, she begins each day at 5:30 A.M. with a two-hour workout at the gym before rehearsals. This need for commitment is well captured in the old joke about the tourist asking someone on the streets of New York City, "How do you get to Carnegie Hall?" The answer of course is, "Practice, practice, practice." Whatever your passion might be, the critical question is whether you have the discipline to see it through.

* * *

The nightingale's passion and talent are to sing. Therefore even when it is deprived of things that are very important, such as freedom and the outdoors, it continues to sing.

Talent and passion are not just the topic of fairy tales, however. In his bestseller *Good to Great*, the business scholar Jim Collins shows that both are essential to outstanding workplace performance. They are necessary for anyone who wants to move from mediocrity to nightingale-level mastery. Jim Collins invites us to think about two important questions: "What do I care about passionately enough that I will aim for greatness?" and "What do I care about enough that I will have the drive and discipline to see it through?" These questions are a great place to start if you want to give more than a perfunctory performance and genuinely give of yourself.

My passion is to help people be authentic and alive in their work, to have a genuine work *life*. My hope is that *The Nightingale,* my own favorite story, has touched you with its song, so that "you may be joyful—and thoughtful."

SOMETHING TO THINK ABOUT...

What scatters your energy, what distracts you from your source of power, and what do you need to say "no" to?

How big a factor are position, perks, and popularity in your work-life choices? How big a factor is your passion and talent?

SOMETHING TO TALK TO YOUR COLLEAGUES ABOUT...

Who are the "nightingales" you enjoy?

What activities and interactions drain us and which ones bring us alive?

NOTES

Introduction

1. Johannes Møllehave, H. C. Andersens salt: Om humoren i H. C. Andersens eventyr (Viborg, Denmark: Lindhardt og Ringhof, 1988), pp. 25–26.

Chapter 1: The Emperor's New Clothes

1. M. Lieberman, "Hurt Feelings Truly Hurt," Science, October 2003.
2. The structure underlying the concepts of a "performer," a "personal manager," and our "essence" is inspired by the work of Carl Jung about the Persona, the Ego, and the Self.

Chapter 2: The Ugly Duckling

1. H. Topsøe-Jensen, Buket til H. C. Andersen (Copenhagen: G.E.C. Gad, 1971), pp. 75–76.
2. Stephen C. Lundin, "Fish Philosophy," FranklinCovey 9th Annual Symposium, Salt Lake City, Utah, October 25, 2002.
3. Interview with Jonathan Young, founding curator, Joseph Campbell Archives, in "Joseph Campbell Centennial," Santa Barbara News Press, March 21, 2004, p. A18.

Chapter 3: The Dung Beetle

1. Jens Andersen, Andersen: En biographi (Copenhagen: Gyldendal, 2003), p. 212.

2. Lance Armstrong, *It's Not About the Bike* (New York: Berkley, 2000), pp. 54–55.

Chapter 5: The Fir Tree

1. Elias Bredsdorf, *Hans Christian Andersen: A Biography* (London: Souvenir Press, 1975), p. 177.
2. Jackie Wullschlager, *Hans Christian Andersen: The Life of a Storyteller* (Chicago: University of Chicago Press, 2000), p. 256.
3. Ibid, p. 258.
4. Richard Tomkins, "Old Father Time Becomes a Terror," *Financial Times*, March 20, 1999, Weekend, p. 1.
5. Anthony Robbins, *Awaken the Giant Within* (New York: Fireside, 1992), p. 28.
6. Dean Harry Lewis, *Slow Down: Getting More out of Harvard by Doing Less* (Cambridge, Mass.: *Harvard College Parents Newsletter*, Fall 2001), p. 1 (abbreviated version of a letter sent to incoming freshmen in August 2001).

Chapter 6: The Nightingale

1. Pablo Zinger, "A Composer Who Found Strength in an Inner Vision," *New York Times*, August 29, 1999, p. 23.
2. Harold Wolff, "The Great G.M. Mystery," *Harvard Business Review*, September–October 1964.
3. Mihaly Csikszentmihalyi, *Flow: The Psychology of Optimal Experience* (New York: Harper Centennial, 1990), p. 226.

ACKNOWLEDGMENTS

IN MY EARLY TEENS I bicycled to school, and it made a world of difference whether I had a headwind or a tailwind. On this book I have received so much support that it felt like a tailwind all the way.

My professional and personal friends and my family have helped me with their encouragement, insights, and advice. Though most are not mentioned by name, please know that I am sincerely grateful. Still a few must be mentioned: Pam Walsh and Carolyn Steigmeier, who nurtured the tender seed of the concept; Margaret Wheatley and Roice Krueger, who advised me to write for everyone in the workplace; June Hopkins and Jonathan Young for their love of fairy tales and advice on Jungian psychology; and Dorthe Nørgaard and Craig Pace for their honest comments on the manuscript.

My thanks also to Consul General Michael Mørch and to the Attaché for Cultural Affairs, Irene Krarup, both at the Danish Consulate in New York, who have championed the book as an official part of the 200-year birthday celebration for Hans Christian Andersen.

As if the creative process of writing a book were not challenging enough, the business of bringing it to market is also daunting. I am grateful to Greg Link and Stephen M. R. Covey, trusted advisers and agents, who caught the vision and provided critical guidance. I am also delighted with the enthusiasm the publishing team at the American Management Association has shown for the project, and a special thanks goes to my editors Jacquie Flynn and Niels Buessem, whose advice made the book better.

Three people deserve special mention. Joan Robins agonized with me over every word of the translation in her vivacious, meticulous, and persistent manner. Flemming Flyvholm helped me express my voice in writing; he reviewed every draft, and I could always count on his warm, thoughtful, and professional guidance. My husband Alfredo Sanchez Gomez shared the ups and downs every step of the way. He was my strongest critic and fiercest supporter, and he continually challenged my ideas and helped me express them more clearly. I feel fortunate to share with him a passion for learning and for expressing who we are in our work.

INDEX

ABOUT THE AUTHOR

DR. METTE NORGAARD is a consultant, teacher, and coach. She has worked with *Fortune* 500 companies, major agencies, entrepreneurial firms, health systems, and professional associations in Europe and the United States.

Dr. Norgaard facilitates workshops and strategy sessions for leadership teams, engaging their best thinking, energy, and commitment. She also leads retreats where participants use timeless stories to think deeply about their professional choices.

Norgaard's background includes being a senior consultant for FranklinCovey and director of the firm's one-week executive retreat. She has also worked as a line leader in healthcare and in manufacturing. Norgaard holds a BA in physical therapy from Aarhus University, Denmark; an MBA from California Lutheran University; and a Ph.D. in human and organizational development from the Fielding Graduate Institute.

Norgaard lives with her husband in New York City.

For more information please go to www.mettenorgaard.com.